Sleeping in the Valley

by

Madeline S. Hoge

Sleeping in the Valley

by Madeline S. Hoge

Sunnyside Cemetery 2020

"As Long As Our Stories Live, We Live." —Old Irish Proverb

Eagle at Sunnyside, 2020

To my loving husband and three boys.

Like two eagles soar as one upon the river of the wind with the promise of forever, we will take the past and learn how to begin.
—Pocahontas

Sleeping in the Valley
Copyright ©2021 by Hayfield Homestead, LLC.

Revised 2022

All Rights Reserved. No part of this book may be used or reproduced in any way without written permission except in the case except in the case of brief quotations embodied in critical articles or reviews.

ISBN: 978-1-7372677-0-6 (paperback)
ISBN: 978-1-7372677-2-0 (hardcover)
ISBN: 978-1-7372677-1-3 (e-book)

For information contact: madeline@belle-hampton.com
Belle-Hampton: www.belle-hampton.com

Paperback | Hardcover | E-book

Contents

Hoge Family Crest..*ix*
Listen to the Mockingbird...*x*
Acknowledgments..*xiii*
Preface ....*xvii*

Chapter 1: Journey Over the Mountain 1
   Sunnyside
   Joseph Samuel Howe b. 1720 d. March 4, 1794 (74 years)
   Ellen Elinor Dunbar Howe b. 1730 d. June 26, 1790 (60 years).......................*xxiv*

Chapter 2: New Beginnings 9
   James Mayo Hoge b. January 12, 1742 d. April 5, 1812 (70 years)..................... 8
   Elizabeth Howe Hoge b. May 10, 1750 d. July 11, 1835 (85 years)................... 11
   Charlotte W. Hoge Trollinger b. January 8, 1813
      d. September 21, 1835 (22 years).. 16, 17

Chapter 3: Romance In the Air... 21
   Major Daniel Howe b. Sep. 20, 1758 d. Jan. 2, 1838 (79 years) 20
   Nancy Heavin Howe b. Jan. 8, 1771 d. March 1, 1830 (59 years)..................... 23

Chapter 4: Where the Weeping Willows Wave 31
   John Brawley Hoge b. Jun 24, 1772 d. Jun 24, 1847 (75 years)........................ 30
   Elizabeth Rippy Hoge b. Jan 12, 1782 d. May 9, 1851 (69 years)..................... 33
   Charlie Hoge b. Jan 22, 1846 d. Jun 8, 1847 (1 year)..35
   Elizabeth M. Hoge b. Jan 14, 1851 d. Feb 14, 1854 (3 years)............................35

Chapter 5: Tis Only Noble to Be Good.. 39
   General James Hoge b. Jul 23, 1783 d. Jul 29, 1861 (78 years)................... 38, 42
   Eleanor Haven Howe b. Dec 1, 1792 d. Jun 13, 1856 (63 years)...................... 43

Chapter 6: Let the Little Children Come to Me 49
William H. Cecil b. Sept. 14, 1850 d. Oct. 7, 1850 (1 month) 48
Julia Ann Cecil b. Feb. 15, 1852 d. Feb. 15, 1854 (2 years) 51

Chapter 7: Our Little Ones 55
Agnes Shannon De Jarnette b. Dec. 15, 1882 d. Jan. 15, 1885 (2 years) 54

Chapter 8: Not My Will But Thine Be Done 59
Eleanor "Nellie" Howe Tyler b. August 28, 1884 d. April 15, 1886 (1 year) 58

Chapter 9: The Reaper and the Flowers 65
Agnes Shannon b. June 15, 1851 d. July 14, 1852 (1 year) 64
John (Johnny) Howe Shannon b. December 6, 1853
  d. June 14, 1877 (23 years) 67, 68

Chapter 10: Wait for the Wagon 71
Maj. John Dunbar Howe b. January 4, 1801 d. January 9, 1885 (84 years) 70
Sarah Boyd Logan Shepherd Howe b. August 20, 1815
  d. March 22, 1859 (43 years) 73
Daniel H. Howe b. June 22, 1831 d. January 6, 1833 (1 year) 75
William Harvey Howe b. August 10, 1849 d. November 10, 1857 (8 years) 76
Samuel Shepherd Howe b. August 16, 1844, d. August 14, 1864 (19 years) 79

Chapter 11: War Is More Bearable Than Peace 85
Ellen Dunbar Howe b. May 6, 1870 d. December 8, 1870 (7 months) 84
Bessie De Jarnette Howe b. December 17, 1871
  d. November 17, 1874 (2 years) 87

Chapter 12: A Life of Service, Knowledge, and Family 93
Dr. William and Jane Hoge 92
Dr. William Edward Hoge b. May 26, 1822 d. Feb. 3, 1885 (62 years) 95
Jane Meek Hoge b. May 12, 1825 d. May 7, 1894 (68 years) 97
Eleanor (Ellen) Justina Hoge b. Jul. 16, 1845
  d. Sep. 16, 1853 (8 years, 2 months) 98
Eliza Hoge b. Oct. 25, 1851 d. Nov. 21, 1851 (27 days) 99

"Still Think of Me," poem by Eliza Hoge (Tyler) 103

Hoge Family Crest painted by Robert H. Hoge, the General's Great Grandson

"Dat Gloria Vires"
A good name gives strength.

Listen to the Mockingbird
Alice Hawthorne

I'm dreaming now of Hally, sweet Hally, sweet Hally,
I'm dreaming now of Hally,
For the thought of her is one that never dies;
She's sleeping in the valley, the valley, the valley,
She's sleeping in the valley,
And the mocking bird is singing where she lies

CHORUS
Listen to the mocking bird,
Listen to the mocking bird,
The mocking bird still singing o'er her grave;
Listen to the Mocking bird,
Listen to the mocking bird,

Still singing where the weeping willows wave.
Ah! Well I yet remember, remember, remember,
Ah! Well I yet remember
When we gather'd in the cotton side by side;
'Twas in the mild September, September, September,
'Twas in the mild September,
And the mocking bird was singing far and wide.
When the charms of spring awaken, awaken, awaken,
When the charms of spring awaken,
And the mocking bird is singing on the bough,
I feel like one forsaken, forsaken, forsaken,
I feel like one forsaken,
Since my Hally is no longer with me now.

QUARTETTE
Listen to the mocking bird,
Listen to the mocking bird,
The mocking bird still singing o'er her grave;
Listen to the mocking bird,
Listen to the mocking bird,
Still singing where the weeping willows wave.
Listen to the mocking bird,
Listen to the mocking bird, the mocking bird still sing
o'er her grave;
Listen to the mocking bird,
Listen to the mocking bird,
Still singing where the weeping willows wave.

    —Hawthorne, Alice, "Listen to the Mocking Bird" (1850).
     Historic Sheet Music Collection.

First visit to Belle-Hampton, Wendy and John Naylor with Peyton Hoge in 2013

Acknowledgment

IN THE BEGINNING, my sister-in-law, Wendy Hoge Naylor, also a historic preservationist, started on a quest to find the elusive family property, Belle-Hampton. Tucked away in the valley, seemingly frozen in time, she found the boarded-up house of General James Hoge, a great-great-great-grandfather. Susan Duerson, a cousin through the General's grandson, Governor James Hoge Tyler, graciously gave Wendy access to her property. It is hard to express my gratitude for my sisters-in-law's diligence to uncover this family treasure. Although her brother, my husband, Tom Hoge, once questioned the purpose of her first visit, we are forever grateful for her interest and resourcefulness to make contact with the Duerson family. With Susan and her son, Brad Duerson, we heard the stories about the people who lived on the property and those buried in Sunnyside's family cemetery. I want to thank them for being stewards of Belle-Hampton for so many years and keeping it in the family by selling the farm to us.

Owned by the neighbor, the cemetery did not get discovered on that first visit of Wendy's. The determination of a young man and budding historian, Patrick Seay, found the hidden, overgrown worn cemetery via satellite maps. Guided by the neighbor's property manager, they found the location where he placed a flag to honor his relative's graves. Knowing the site, we were later granted access to clear, clean, and maintain the cemetery. My thanks to Patrick for understanding the importance of honoring the lives of those buried at Sunnyside. And to R. J. Kirk and his family to allow access to maintain the site.

For all of the strenuous and time-consuming work to clean and clear the cemetery, my appreciation goes to my husband, Tom Hoge. From the first tedious cut of the thick weeds to the resurrecting of the gravestones, his hard labor did not go unnoticed. Sunnyside became transformed into a place of honor for the buried souls due to his effort. Our boys, Tyler, Peyton, and Mason Hoge, along with him, helped with the endless growth from season to season. Hot, humid days did not keep all of them from toiling away to get the cemetery ready for family visitors to celebrate the dead on July 4th.

This book would not be possible without the photographic documentation compiled by my brother-in-law, John Naylor. From his very first visit, he captured the moments of exploration into the historic property. On other visits, he recorded the progress of the restoration. When I asked if he would creatively take pictures of all of the graves, he obliged. The photographs, without exception, turned out phenomenally. He has a keen eye to capture both casual portraits of people and static structures such as gravestones. As you browse through this book, note that all of the pictures are his, including my author's photo. I truly appreciate all of his time and effort to take, edit and compile the images. Thank you.

This collection of stories about the lives of those buried here included research of well-documented families, the Hoges and Howes. The purpose is never to forget our ancestors' lives and the values passed along from generation to generation.

> *People will not look forward to posterity who never look backward to their ancestors.*
> —Burke

But my research would not be possible without my "go-to" historian, April Martin. We first met April at Smithfield in Blacksburg when we wandered in for a tour. When introduced, she immediately recognized the name, knowing we purchased Belle-Hampton from her research. Since then, she has been an enormous resource, from identifying gravestone markings to coaching us on proper cleaning and preserving cemeteries. The Wilderness Museum, where she now works, has a large records room and library, which provided some of the information for this book. However, April's vast knowledge gave me insight into the era in which these families lived. From explaining the Battle of Cloyd's Mountain to deciphering old handwriting in ledgers, she has been a constant source of valuable information. I appreciate how much she has helped this novice hobby historian.

Thanks to my sisters, Carlene Szostak and Charlotte McLaughlin, who helped me through the ins and outs of book writing and publishing. Together, we published a children's book, *The Marshmallow Mystery*, under the penname CJ Corki. Through that experience, I became inspired to complete my book, which I worked on for well over a year before publishing the children's book.

My thanks to everyone for your support in my mission to preserve the history of Belle-Hampton farm and the families who spent their lives on the property. And once again, I would like to thank my husband and boys for helping me live *intentionally.*

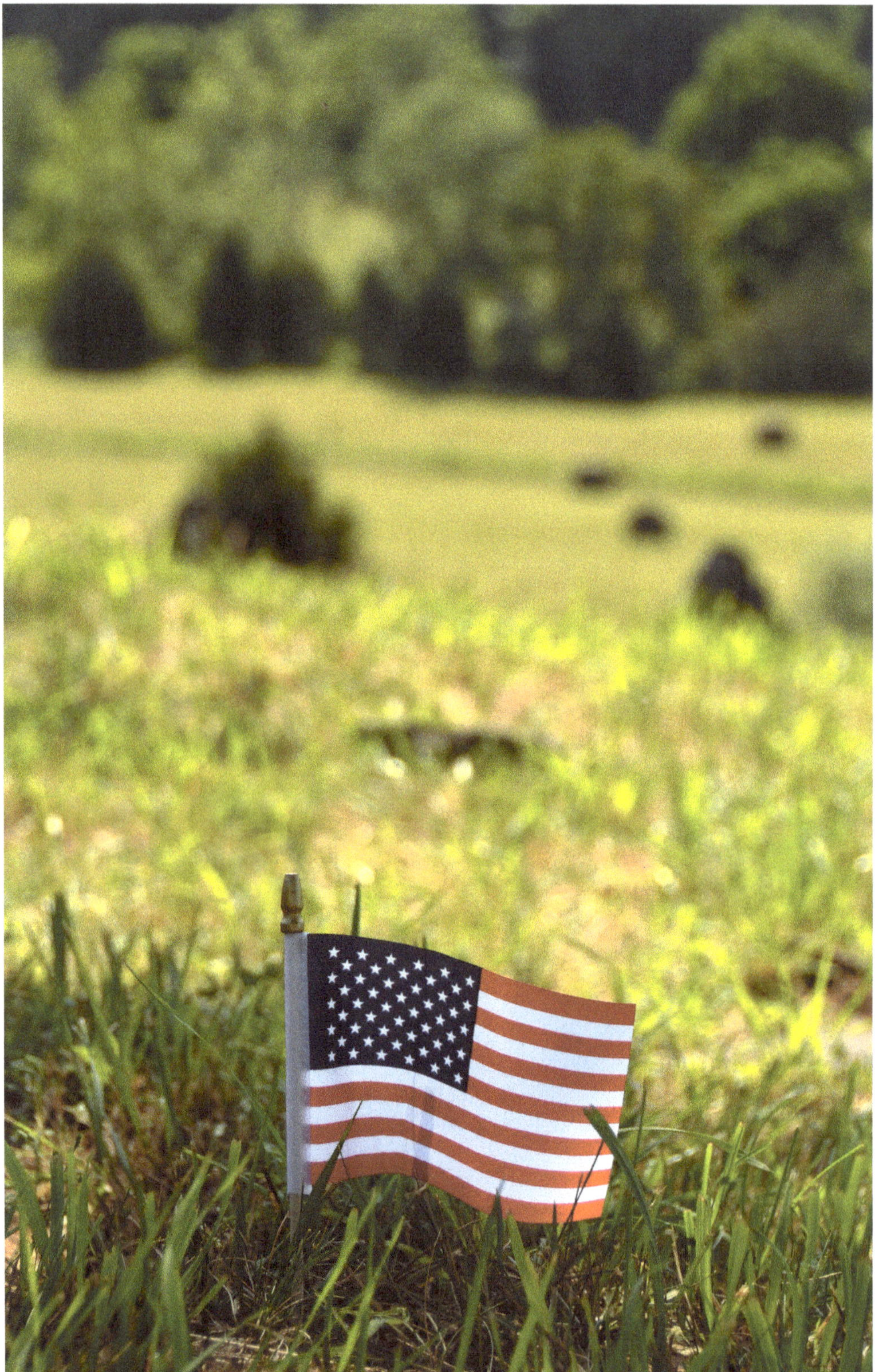

Preface

Then join hand in hand, brave Americans all,
By uniting we stand, by dividing we fall;
In so righteous a cause let us hope to succeed,
For heaven approves of each generous deed.

—*The Liberty Song,* John Dickinson, 1768

TO UNDERSTAND THE LIFE STORIES of those buried in the Sunnyside Cemetery, Pulaski County, VA, we need to begin with a brief history of the families. Prominent names such as De Jarnette, Shannon, Cecil, and Trollinger are all buried there; however, the principal families we will be discussing at length are the Hoge and Howe families, whose descendants are intertwined. Both the Hoges and the Howes were the progenitors of their family in the New River Valley. Joseph Howe was engaged in blazing the Catawba trail in 1750 and moved to Sunnyside shortly after, along with James Mayo Hoge. But their families came across the pond much earlier.

William Hoge was the first in America in 1682. William was born into the Scottish nobility, which instilled in him the importance of his good name's strength. However, even with a strong character and suitable means, William ended up in jail. It was not for a crime but for his beliefs and strong religious convictions. He was a strict Covenanter, a person who pledged to uphold Presbyterianism. But his strong principles would test his strength and bravery.

During this period, England was acquiring land in America and taking it from the Scottish. The Stuarts, reigning monarchs in England and Scotland, also wanted everyone to believe in the king's book, also called the Book of Common Prayer. William would not conform to the ruler's decree. He had his possessions taken away and was stripped of his nobility. William now sat rotting in jail, left to change his beliefs or die.

Life in jail required determination and character. Did William believe his good name would give him strength, as said by the motto on their family coat of arms, *Dat gloria vires?* He could have conformed to the king's belief, which would have set him free, but he chose to hold true to his convictions even if it meant enduring the severe conditions of prison. His brothers were also subject to persecution for their beliefs. The family withstood the pressure to conform to the Stuart dynasty's religion, although they had to endure personal condemnation.

Fortunately, William could be freed from jail if he were to leave the country. The story goes that Sir James, William's father, had a brother who conformed to the king's book, who pulled some strings to get him freed. The ship *Caledonia,* the Latin name for Scotland, was headed for America. William's options were limited. Either start a new life in America or stay in jail. He took the challenge, boarding the crowded, run-down ship full of Scottish prisoners going to a foreign land.

Caledonia was not a festive cruise ship but a rat-infested, poorly built boat with rotting wood. The ship, crowded with prisoners from war or religious prosecution, indentured servants, and gypsies, left for the new world. The voyage took months, with waves battering the ship as it tossed around in the rough waters of the North Atlantic Ocean. They had little food, supplies, or medical services. It is not surprising that disease struck the passengers, with half dying on the journey from either pestilence or malnutrition. The vessel sprung a leak but eventually ran ashore into Perth Amboy, NJ. Once on dry land, their adventure in America began.

Unfortunately, the beginning looked grim. William arrived penniless in a strange land. A fellow passenger, Barbara Hume, lost her parents on the ship from an epidemic, leaving her at the young age of 12 alone in a new world. William, who was 10 years older, became her protector. William made sure Barbara reached her mother's family, the Johnsons, in New York. He delivered her and her property to her uncle before returning to Perth Amboy to work for a Scottish company and make himself a home.

Since travel was expensive and challenging at the time, even though New York was only 28 miles away for William, the contact between the pair must have been limited. But, somehow, an attachment sprung up between them. After six years, William returned to marry Barbara in around 1688. After the birth of their first son, John, they moved to Pennsylvania.

William was attracted to Pennsylvania's new colony, which gave him religious freedom and opportunity in a growing community. William Penn, the founder of Pennsylvania, had created a government with the goal of religious tolerance. He started the "holy experiment," which allowed for religious freedom. He hoped his advertisements would attract people so he could "seed the nation."

William Hoge purchased 1,000 acres of land in Chester County, Pennsylvania, for five shillings with additional quit rent, a land tax, to William Penn for 15 years. Pennsylvania was a booming area for settlers because of the waterways and stagecoach trails. Philadelphia was the third-largest city in America and was rich in culture. As the colony was developing, Hoge sold pieces of his land to the new settlers.

By age 75, William still had not reached his full potential and decided to move his wife and nine children to Kernstown, Virginia's remote wilderness. After 20 years of hard work and selling his property in Pennsylvania, William was now debt-free and able to buy more land. However, his oldest son, John, stayed in the Pennsylvania area since his wife Gwenthleum, part of the royal family of Wales, sold her royal jewelry so they could purchase a large tract of land to build their home. John proceeded to found Hogestown, PA, near Harrisburg and built a church for the community.

Since England was promoting Virginia's beauty and vast land availability to settlers, William and Barbara took the risk to head west. The English government wanted to encourage this westward expansion to dispel what they saw as savage Indians who were massacring the new inhabitants. Before the growth, only trappers, traders, and explorers made it to the Shenandoah Valley. Through a land grant, 16 families were able to make Virginia their home (Glass, Vance, Allen, Reed, Colville, White, Marquis, Beckett, Chambers, McAuley, McMachen and others). Among them were the Hoge family. William received a patent from the colony of Virginia for 411 acres in 1735. He secured the land in Winchester, VA, near a main traveling route.

Location, location, location is typically essential in real estate. The land that William secured was along a well-traveled route where he then opened an ordinary. An ordinary was a tavern, and an essential part of the community. It was a place for food and drink as well as a place to stay. Along the stagecoach route, travelers would stop and have lunch, typically included in their fare. Sandwiches became the first fast foods that people could take along with them on the stagecoach.

However, the ordinary served as more than just a place to eat. The local people would gather here to talk about issues of the day and legislative matters. Ordinaries sometimes had more business conducted in them than the official meeting houses. They also served as a post office, recruitment office, and place of deployment of the militia. It was common to have an ordinary close to a church, so it is not surprising that William sold (or donated) some of his lands for the first meeting house, which was to be the first church in the area.

Opequon Presbyterian Church started meeting in 1732 during the Great Awakening, a period of religious revival. They may have held their meetings in Hoge's ordinary. In 1736, they built a meeting house on William's land and with his materials. William's grandson, Rev. John Hoge, was in the first class from Nassau Hall, Princeton. John was the first minister of the church. The story is that George Washington would often attend the church and then dine with Nancy Hoge Wilson, William's daughter. Unfortunately, the original church was destroyed and rebuilt several times over the years and any evidence of the story's validity lost. Therefore, we cannot officially say that George Washington prayed there.

After being raised in nobility and good circumstances, William Hoge had to endure being stripped of his possessions, imprisoned, and relocated to uncharted territories, but seemed to make the best of his situation. Though he went without knowing his own hopes and dreams, he created a legacy in America with his good name and sound values. From him sprung a branch of the family, scattered from New York to California. These were men of substance and character: bankers, lawyers, judges, members of Congress, and now and then a minister of the Gospel; they were leaders in church and state. Buried at the Opequon Church Cemetery, William and Barbara leave the ancestral dynasty of the Hoge name in keeping with their motto, *Dat gloria vires,* "a good name gives strength."

Joseph Samuel Howe came to America approximately 55 years after William Hoge. In 1737, he left his home in Nottinghamshire, England, shortly after his father died. He was the oldest son of Sir Emanuel Scrope Howe, 2nd Viscount Howe, 4th Baronet of Compton. His grandmother, Sophia von Kielmansegg, Countess of Darlington, was the half sister of King George I. Rumor had it that she was one of his mistresses, which his mother strongly dismissed. However, whether the king's children were actually from Sophia was still in question. Countess Sophia was undoubtedly a close confidant of the king since she lived in the palace before her marriage. Her oldest daughter, Charlotte, was Howe's mother. Being raised in nobility with connections to the crown, his reason for leaving home is unclear; he was only 17. Allegedly, he ran away to be with his younger brother, Brigadier General George Augustus Howe, 3rd Viscount

Howe. The latter was serving in the French and Indian War in America. Unfortunately, his brother died in the Battle of Ticonderoga in 1758.

During the Revolutionary War (1775–83), fought by the American colonies to gain independence from Great Britain, another one of Howe's brothers, Sir William Howe, was formally appointed commander in chief of the British Army in America in 1775. Stating that "he was ordered, and could not refuse," General William Howe sailed for Boston with major generals Henry Clinton and John Burgoyne. Howe led a successful Battle of Bunker Hill defeating the inexperienced colonists under Colonel William Prescott. George Washington was put in charge of the American Revolution three weeks later. Howe, soon joined by another brother Richard, had orders to act as a peace commissioner. On September 11, 1776, the Howes met with John Adams, Benjamin Franklin, and Edward Rutledge on Staten Island. The American representatives mandated recognition of their independence, but the Howes were only permitted to offer pardons to those rebels who submitted to British authority. The Howe's efforts failed, and the hope of peace without any more bloodshed became impossible.

General William Howe later defeated George Washington at Long Island and New York, thus capturing New York City and making it his headquarters. In 1777, after various successful battles against the colonists, William asked to be relieved of his position. He was brought to the House of Commons for a review of his conduct, but this proved to be inconclusive. Why did he step down from his duty during the Revolution? It is curious since, at that point in time, his brother Joseph Howe, referred to earlier, was working with George Washington building forts for the French and Indian War, later serving as a "road viewer" for the colonists in the Revolutionary War. But Richard and William Howe stayed loyal to England, continuing their duties though they both opposed war with the colonies.

Joseph Samuel Howe left his privileged life in England to forge unknowingly into the wilderness of America. Coming from a home of refinement and wealth with strong convictions and connections to the crown, it seems curious he would have taken on such a risky adventure. Speculating his motivations, Howe may have forfeited a royal title in exchange for land in the new world. Since he sympathized with the American colonists, maybe it was perceived intolerable back at home with his family. His first trip at 17 might have opened his eyes to the opportunities in the new world, and he may have jumped on the offer of land in exchange for the privileges of nobility. The truth of this refined gentleman's inspirations to venture into the wilderness is a mystery; however, the legacy he left in America lives on.

These two distinguished families, Hoge and Howe, had a vision for a life beyond themselves. Through perseverance and strength of character, they now lie in the family cemetery hidden from the world. But as the old Irish proverb states, "As long as our stories live, we live." Enjoy the life stories of these souls now buried at the Sunnyside Cemetery.

Sunnyside, 2017
Joseph Samuel Howe b. 1720 d. March 4, 1794 (74 years)
Ellen Elinor Dunbar Howe b. 1730 d. June 26, 1790 (60 years)

CHAPTER 1

Journey Over the Mountain

Chester

Let the high heav'ns your songs invite,
These spacious fields of brilliant light,
Where sun and moon and planets roll,
And stars that glow from pole to pole.

Sun, moon, and stars convey Thy praise,
'Round the whole earth and never stand,
So when Thy truth began its race,
It touched and glanced on ev'ry hand.

— William Billings during the Revolutionary War

LOST IN THE GRAVEYARD WITHOUT A STONE are the oldest documented graves in the Sunnyside Cemetery, Major Joseph Howe and his wife, Ellen Elinor Dunbar Howe. The family would like to recognize these early adventurers and first settlers of the New River Valley in the cemetery with new markers. Still, until then, they are left unadorned, surrounded by heroic and accomplished descendants.

Major Joseph Howe was the founder of the Howe family in America. According to the family legend told through generations, he ran away from his home in England to join his brother, Lord George Augustus Howe, who was one of the English officers fighting in the French and Indian War. Supposedly, he arrived about the time his brother died at the

Battle of Ticonderoga, 1758. However, we now know that Joseph Howe reached the Northern Virginia frontier as early as 1749. George Washington's journal of land surveys made along the Lost River of the Cacapon recorded his activities in this region that year.

The record confirms that a "Joseph How" accompanied George Washington on the survey of his tract of land and assisted by marking the trees designated by the young surveyor as the boundary line and corner trees of the land grant. The land surveys are recorded in detail in Washington's diary, in which he recounts his day-by-day experience through the Lost River region.

George Washington appreciated the Howes and the other settlers for making room for him in their homes. The accommodation would best be described as a spartan hand-hewn log cabin since they were the only structures in the Virginia frontier mountains at the time. It most likely was so crowded that Washington had to sleep on a deerskin rug on the floor tucked in front of a warm fire. If Howe's log cabin were still standing, it would surely be home to boasts that "George Washington once slept here."

In a further experience with George Washington, Howe had his first military adventure under Washington's command around 1751 while living in northern Augusta County. The Northern Virginia frontier became so threatened by the hostile Shawnee Indians, allied with the French against the pioneers, that all men were called to become part of a militia for protection against the raids. According to history, George Washington, who studied military tactics, was placed in charge of preparing a defense for the district headquarters in Frederick Town. At the time, pioneers received land to build forts and stockades for protection and attract additional settlers. Fortifications along the Rappahannock River were the only safeguard for pioneers in this raw territory. Frequent meetings with Washington in the field were a certainty during this time before and during the French and Indian War. This North American conflict was part of a larger imperial war between Great Britain and France known as the Seven Years' War.

In 1756 after the official French and Indian War was declared, Joseph Howe and John Dunbar (his father-in-law), along with other settlers living at Fort Riddle, presumably took part in a battle against the French and Indians. Fifty Indian warriors led by a French officer were preying on frontier settlers. Captain Jeremiah Smith decided to raise a militia of 20 men to intercept the attackers near Lost River (now Hardy County, West Virginia). Fighting between the two sides was fierce; however, the militia prevailed. Unfortunately, detailed recordings about the campaign and the names of the militia soldiers are missing. Still, Howe's participation in the battle can be substantiated by the legend of the "curious metal tag," assumed removed from an Indian's nose during this fight. The French supplied the Indians with these tags to recognize them as allies during the war. Proudly displayed on the mantel in Howe's home at Sunnyside, the tale of the battle was passed along for generations. George Washington presented Major Howe with an elaborately decorated silver sword for his services during the war, including his help to fortify the wilderness. Regrettably, his great-granddaughter melted the silver down to make a silver cup for her son.

Joseph Howe's first encounter with John Dunbar and his family most likely happened on a voyage to America. There is speculation that Howe crossed back over the pond several times, so the exact meeting date is unknown. Elinor (Ellen), Dunbar's only child of record, and Joseph were married around 1754 in Boston shortly before migrating to the northern part of the Virginia colony, Hampshire County (now West Virginia).

Howe had taken part in blazing the Catawba Trail in 1750, so he was familiar with the early settlers' southern route. The Catawba Trail was part of the network of trails blazed through the virgin land. Enchanted with the scenic rolling mountains and rivers during these trips to the New River Valley, he decided he would someday live in Montgomery County, Virginia (now Pulaski County).

In 1767, he disposed of his land in Hampshire County and made the 200-mile trek with his wife and six young children. His oldest son, Joseph, died young before their journey. Their oldest daughter, Elizabeth, was only 16 years old, John, 14 years, Ann, 11 years, Daniel, 9 years, and Rebecca, only 2 years. Elinor most likely was pregnant during the move since she delivered her youngest, David, during that same year. These roads were primitive and dangerous; there was jungle-like growth in the flat terrain, and traversing the Blue Ridge Mountains was especially problematic. As the Howe family caravanned their way in 10-foot by 4-foot covered wagons at a rate of approximately 20 miles a day, they were in constant fear of hostile Indians, wild animals, and the hot August heat. Once they sighted the lush green hillside and the sparkling blue creek, their relief turned to exuberance as they eyed the log home waiting for them.

The presumption was that Howe built the log cabin shortly after securing the land grant in 1758 in preparation for his family's arrival. He created this log cabin to temporarily accommodate and protect his family at their destination in the wilderness. Located on a south-facing knoll by a natural spring, Howe aptly named it "Sunnyside." After a few years, Howe built a more expansive log cabin to fit his large family, which he located about a mile down the stream on the north side of Back Creek. Keeping with tradition, the name "Sunnyside" still refers to the home that exists there today.

Since many of the settlers left their country of origin due to religious persecution, Joseph Howe and many others in the New River Valley were devoted followers of their ancestors' Presbyterian faith. Naturally, one of the first concerns of these pioneers was to establish a place of worship. In 1768, Hanover Presbytery, defined as those who favored the aggressive evangelism and itinerant preaching associated with the First Great Awakening, sent the Reverend John Craig on a mission to Western Virginia's frontier to organize the Presbyterians settled there into various congregations. One of the eight churches Rev. Craig organized on his missionary journey of 1768–69 was at New Dublin's settlement. No other Protestant community is known to have existed "on the western waters," or west of the Alleghenies, before Rev. Craig organized the New Dublin congregation. On April 13, 1769, Rev. Craig estimated that 45 families were able to pay 45 pounds sterling toward the support of a minister at New Dublin. The meeting minutes also list the first elders of the congregation, whom Rev. Craig had probably ordained. They were Joseph Howe, Samuel Colville, John Taylor, Samuel Cloyd, and James Montgomery. These elders sent a formal appeal to the presbytery for a supply pastor. The minutes of this presbytery meeting contain the oldest known written reference to New Dublin Presbyterian Church. There is no record of the congregation erecting a church building at the New Dublin village; the assembly most likely held services in churchgoers' homes in the church's earliest days. Until 1773, Samuel's cousin Joseph Cloyd, who owned 4,000 acres, donated some of his lands to the church in an attempt to persuade his bride, Elizabeth Gordon, to move to the area. She feared for her safety having heard the stories of the Indian raids which killed Joseph's mother and brother. For her, a church brought a sense of civility to the area. She agreed to the move, but he wasn't able to immediately fulfill his promise. The church did not get built until after the Revolutionary War as all able-bodied men were enlisted to fight for their freedom.

During the Revolutionary War, Joseph Howe served as a "road viewer." This role was key since he was responsible for making sure roads were surveyed and cleared for the troops. If the British interfered with road passage for some reason, Howe was to remove or handle the disruption. After the war, Howe lived a long and contented life at Sunnyside, his paradise. He continually added to his home while clearing acres for crops, vineyards, and orchards. He accumulated more livestock and other assets through the years until he passed at a ripe old age of 74.

Howe's appearance or characteristics are undocumented, but knowing he was from a distinguished English family, he was presumed to have an elegant courtly manner—best described as a gentleman with an adventurous spirit. He died in March of 1794. His will quotes the following:

> "In the name of God, Amen—I, Joseph Howe, of the County of Montgomery, being of perfect mind and memory and calling to mind the uncertainty of life and that it is appointed for all men once to die, therefore, first of all, I recommend my spirit unto God that gave it and my body to the Earth, trusting and believing through the mercy of God and the complete satisfaction of Jesus Christ, my redeemer, to receive it at the general resurrection. And what worldly estate it hath pleased God in his providence to Bless me with, I order to be disposed of in the following manner: First of all, I do direct that my Executor, Daniel Howe, shall keep and maintain my dearly beloved wife, Elinor Howe, for during her natural life, decently and well."

According to the old English law and custom followed in America at that time, the family estate generally passed down to the oldest son. However, their first son, Joseph, died at an early age before their move to Virginia. Their second oldest son, John, secured 400 acres of land in Kentucky, where he married Mary Ann Waggoner and established his family. Major Daniel Howe, the youngest son, became the new owner of Sunnyside on the death of his father.

Curiously, Joseph Howe's wife, Ellen Elinor Dunbar, died at the time of the will's writing. The Dunbars lack documentation about their family before arriving from Scotland. Elinor's father, John Dunbar, traveled to America in the early 1700s, where he married his wife, Mary, in Boston, MA. Shortly after their marriage, Elinor was born, although it is disputed whether this was in Boston, Scotland, or England. Later, the Dunbars secured a land grant in Virginia along with the Howes, which led the Howes and Hoges on the trek into the wilderness.

According to family history, Elinor was medium-sized with light hair and blue eyes. Since she walked with a slight limp, she required a cane. Along with other tales of Sunnyside, supposedly, you can still hear her cane striking the floor as she continues to walk through her homestead. The spirits of Joseph and Elinor Howe may be mere ghosts at Sunnyside;

however, the legends of their lives continue to live on. Descendants of theirs became heroes in war, leaders in politics, successes in business, and acclaimed orators in the region, reflecting Joseph Howe's vision for a new nation. Escaping the trappings of heraldry and the gentile life of the British elite, they embraced liberty to help form America.

In memory of
JAMES HOGE
who departed this life April
5, 1842, aged 70 years, 2
months and 23 days.

CHAPTER 2

New Beginnings

To A Dear Friend

Farewell, my friend, and should we meet no more
While life beats warm within our bosom core,
Let not this last, this warm embrace,
Be from thy memory ere effaced.

Remember how upon this rock we stood.
With wandering eyes and musing mood.
Oh, it was a feast for our admiring eyes
To see those high majestic mountains rise.

The rolling river, as with wonder fired,
Just showed its silver face, and then retired;
With bashful mien it ran away,
While we in vain implored it stay.

—Eliza Hoge (Tyler)
October 4, 1835

Note: Charlotte Hoge Trollinger died right before this was written.

PEACEFULLY RESTING ON A HILL overlooking the fields that he arrived on 45 years before his death, James Mayo Hoge's tomb, distinguished by a slightly crooked, perfectly preserved gravestone, memorializes his passing at age 70. The stone, embellished with an eight-pointed star symbolizing new beginnings, lays next to his loving wife, Elizabeth. Her stone is adorned with a similar design and has all but fallen over from years withstanding the elements. Nearby, Charlotte, their granddaughter, has a mere fragment of a memorial withered to the point of an almost indefinable plaque representing her short life. The stories of their lives were passed down for seven generations along with the hope to remember them for seven more.

James Mayo Hoge (or James Hoge Jr.) grew up in Frederick County, Virginia, about 75 miles west of Washington, D.C. He was one of eight children from his father, James, with his first wife, Ms. Fulton. His dad was "a man of robust intellect and a self-taught theologian, adhering strictly to the Westminster confession." Note, the Westminster Confession was part of the Protestant Reformation; many Scots adhered. But after James Mayo's mother died, his father remarried a much younger woman and had four additional children. Their youngest son evolved into a prestigious minister, Rev. Moses Hoge, D.D.

But the adventurous James Mayo decided it was time to leave home in search for his older brother, John, who was away fighting in the French and Indian War. John enlisted in Braddock's army, whose unit was carving a road to Fort Duquesne, PA, from Fort Cumberland, MD. This 110-mile venture was a logistical challenge since they had to carry equipment through the densely wooded Allegheny Mountains. Besides the notable figure of George Washington, Daniel Boone and Benjamin Franklin also made the trek. Unfortunately, the battle that ensued at Fort Duquesne was a significant loss for the British, and the battle became known as Braddock's Defeat. Although John was thought to be killed in this expedition as documented in the Hoge family book, he actually survived. At some point, he had been captured and taken to France as a prisoner of war. As a captive at the Cognac Castle in Poullignac, he and other inmates carved their names and pictures on the limestone, reminiscent of cave paintings, which are still visible today. Two years later, he wrote a letter home saying he was very much alive.

James obviously failed to find his brother while traveling into the remote wilderness, eventually ending up in Southwest Virginia. During this considerable period of time between looking for his brother and arriving in Virginia, his life history is unaccounted for. Documented evidence shows time spent in Fredricksburg, VA, approximately 100 miles from his home, but no details of his activities. Speculation would believe he joined the battles of war or assisted in the building of forts, but we will never know for sure. His wanderings, however, would have given him time to meet his wife-to-be, Elizabeth Howe, eldest daughter of Joseph and Elinor

Elizabeth Howe Hoge b. May 10, 1750 d. July 11, 1835 (85 years)

Howe, and follow her family further into the remote area of what is now Pulaski County, VA.

We know with certainty that he found his wife from his wanderings and interactions with Joseph Howe, following them to Southwest Virginia. After his marriage at the old Howe homestead called Sunnyside, James made a log and stone cabin of his own in 1767 adjacent to his in-law's farm. He named the homestead Hayfield after a familiar landmark from his childhood in Frederick County. Also, it is reasonable to assume that he may have given the stream near which he and Elizabeth Howe Hoge began their new life the name "Back Creek" after another landmark. After their marriage, but before the Revolutionary War, they had four children, Eleanor, Joseph, John, and Agnes. During his service, there was a lapse of time in which Elizabeth needed to manage the young children and the homestead alone.

Although James settled in the area along with his father-in-law, Joseph Howe, despite orders by king's proclamation not to move into territory past the Allegheny, they justifiably did so to claim the land that was rightfully theirs. But few settlers followed, as their passage was hindered by uncleared thoroughfare. Their homestead became even more isolated from civilization in a dangerous time. Defying British orders was the first show of Southwest Virginians' dissatisfaction with the rulings from the other side of the pond.

In June 1775, James enlisted as a soldier, two months after the Revolutionary War began in Lexington, VA, less than 100 miles away from his home. He served as a private in Captain Hendricks' Company, which fought in the losing expedition against Quebec. Those enlisted abided by their orders to bring "a good firearm, a cartouch box, blanket, and knapsack." They made their own bullets at camp, but boredom soon became their enemy. To keep the soldiers occupied, instead of drills, they were sent to hide out and pick off the redcoats as they marched in formation. But someone, not identified, suggested that George Washington send his troops on a 500-mile trek to Quebec to defeat the redcoats in order to gain support for the anti-British rebellion among the French Canadians that lived there. On their arrival, the snow became deep, and a siege on the city would have been impossible, but they had to advance before the new year. On the night of December 30, to make things worse, the temperatures dropped, and the conditions unexpectedly became more brutal. At 2:00 a.m. on December 31, 1775, under cover of snowfall, General Richard Montgomery and Benedict Arnold led the troops into the city. Hendricks and his company brought up the rear behind Arnold. Although the plan was to surprise the enemy, the British defenders were ready for the Patriots and, under a barrage of artillery and musket fire, killed or captured approximately 400 soldiers. Those men who were second-generation Americans were taken as prisoners of war while the others forcibly served with the British. James, a second-generation American, was held captive at the fortress in Quebec.

Unlike most prisoners of war, who were neglected and considered traitors by the king, they were treated well in captivity, but boredom and disease made conditions difficult. Fortunately, the Jesuits helped with illnesses by comforting the sick and offering medicine or hospital care. A year later, after the Declaration of Independence was signed, the prisoners were released. Twenty-one ragged, weary men from Captain Hendricks' Company headed home in the fall of 1776. Because only the British recorded the affairs, history neglected this small company and their story was never chronicled on their return. Possibly accounting for James's conflicting documentation in the war from 1777–1790, he had been among the first half-dozen units beyond the Hudson to serve.

The Militia of Montgomery County, established from 1777–1790, listed James as a "Patriotic Service Soldier." About 45,000 enlisted in the Virginia Company, but a quarter of them weren't in active duty until 1781 when summoned into service. James's name doesn't appear on the roll until 1781 under the command of Captain Henry Patton. We know his daughter Sara was born in 1780, which matches the timeline. After the tough battle in Quebec and being a prisoner of war, he most likely went home to recover. Patton's Company served in the Battle of Guilford Courthouse which was a significant turning point in the war. James was in active duty at the Battle of Yorktown with the eventual surrender of the British under the command of General Cornwallis. Yorktown was the last major battle in the Revolutionary War, which ended in 1783 with the Treaty of Paris.

After the war, in 1785, James served as a "road viewer" for a passage from the south side of Little Walker's Creek Mountain to Brown's Bottom, which involved establishing a ferry across the new river. Although documents show he still served in the militia, we know James returned to Hayfield, close to the land he was surveying, continuing his family's expansion. James Hoge (who would later become a general) was born after the war ended in 1783; Elizabeth, Mary, Daniel, William, and Martha were born soon after that time.

Being committed to serving the community, in 1795, James Mayo was appointed "overseer" of the poor. This elected position helped people who could not provide for themselves, the equivalent of today's welfare system. Called "Outdoor Relief," the overseer would determine a person's need and allocate money from the government for assistance. When requirements were significant, the person landed at the poorhouse, a tax supported residential institution, not to be confused with debtors' prison. In 1796, James was appointed "commissioner of revenue," his duties requiring him to establish tax policy, set rates, carry out assessments, and determine taxable items. Besides his service to the community, he farmed his land and established a gristmill in 1797.

The oldest son of James and Elizabeth was Joseph Johnson Hoge, who married Barbara Brawley in 1790. James deeded his son 200 acres of land for "love and affection" four years after the marriage, but in 1795, Joseph sold the land to Joseph Cloyd so they could move to Tennessee. The adventurous Hoge saw an opportunity to bring his family to a new territory that needed 60,000 people before becoming a state. Although this new frontier was even more remote and unknown, Joseph was willing to take the risk. It is uncertain whether his wife and family moved there initially since Barbara had three more children born in Virginia.

In 1795, James had an extensive survey made that reflected his land's extent, 305 acres, for an issued land grant. In 1809, his son General James Hoge (captain at that time) purchased 133 acres from his father on Back Creek near Shufflebarger's Mill located east of Route 100 and south of Cloyd's Mountain. The general subsequently married his first cousin, Eleanor, about that same time; however, sources state they may have ben married on June 5, 1810.

On May 18, 1809, James Mayo Hoge, who was 67 years old at the time, wrote his will as follows:

> To his wife Elizabeth, he devised one-third of the plantation for her lifetime and one-third of the personal estate. To his son James, he left the remaining two-thirds of the land he was living on and the entire estate at Elizabeth's death. James was then to pay the other sons as follows: Joseph $5, John $45, Daniel $200, and William $150. James noted that his young daughter Mary was still living at home and was to be equal with all the others who were already married.

Interestingly, James left his estate to the general, who was not the oldest son as it typically would have been in those days. As stated before, we know that their oldest son already received property. John, who would be the next oldest, only received $45 dollars. Although John had already been married three times by the time the will was written, it isn't clear how much land he owned at that time. We do know John had a log cabin built on Neck Creek in 1800. Stories recount how he used the $45 he received at the time of his father's death to purchase land and acquire as much real estate as his brother, 1,012 acres. It can be noted, however, that the general may have bought out his siblings' interests in his father's estate. Since James Mayo had 11 children, the general's portion of the estate would have been minimal. The general and his father may have reached an agreement when he purchased his father's land, which was the same time as the will's writing.

When James Mayo Hoge died in 1812, his estate, appraised by Joseph Reyburn, Richard Guthrie, and Jacob Peck, had the following items listed:

> Hemp, horses, and mares including one horse called Charley Horse, calves, cows, heifers, steers, a bull, 29 hogs, 16 old sheep and six lambs, a loom and weaving utensils, a wool wheel, two plows, a wagon and gears, and a wagon cloth, sithes, two sets if hangings, 6 fallen axes, 12 cedar vessels, two kegs, two pots, one oven, one skillet, one frying pan, pot hooks, pails and buckets, metal sifter, fire tongs, a large kettle, cupboard and furniture, pewter and tinware, looking glass, copper teakettle, ten old chairs, one chest, a desk, candle stand, clock and case, one pair

large money scales, inkstand, steelyards, two slates, books, four beds, 30 pounds of wool, two sheets, shoemaker's box and tools, reel, feathers, five beehives and bees, a stone jug, a Negro man named Amos, a grindstone, and several notes and accounts.

A grindstone, one of two circular stones used for grinding grain or other substances, which passed on to the general is still part of Belle-Hampton, formerly Hayfield, today.

Elizabeth Howe was only a teenager when she met her husband-to-be, James Mayo Hoge. Married at age 18, she devoutly worked side by side with her husband, as did most pioneer women of the day. Elizabeth learned to meet challenges with perseverance and determination, along with caring for children, pregnancy, and raising babies in the austere log cabin they built. After her husband died, as stated in his will, she continued to live at Hayfield. The general bought his mother and siblings out and settled on May 28, 1812, $180 for the estate's appraised value as stated in the general's ledger. This would have been around $3,500 in today's dollar. She lived a long healthy life and passed away presumably from old age at 85. According to his ledger, the general, the estate executor, arranged for a marble headstone and coffin for his mother.

Charlotte, whose grave is near her grandparents, was born nine months after James Mayo Hoge died. She was the oldest child of William and Margaret Anderson Hoge, who married only a year before William's father passed on. How blessed they must have felt during the family's time of loss to bring a new life into the world. Charlotte was named after her great-grandmother, Maria Sophia Charlotte, who was German royalty and the half sister of King George I of England. Charlotte was raised in Pulaski County, Virginia (Montgomery County at the time) with her sisters, Hannah and Elizabeth. The girls were all born within four years of each other and presumed to be very close. Charlotte was married in 1830, with Hannah and Elizabeth getting married in 1831 and 1832, respectively. Soon after, they all began to have children. Charlotte had William (1831) and Henry (1833), while Hannah gave birth in 1832 and 1834. Elizabeth, the youngest sister, moved to Mechanicsburg, VA, and started her family of 11 children there. How proud their grandmother, Elizabeth, would have been to enjoy all these young children in her later years in life.

Charlotte married John Trollinger Jr. at Back Creek in 1830. The Trollinger family had arrived in Dublin while it was still a frontier. The German-born pioneer Henry Jacob Trollinger moved to the area just east of the now Dublin depot to make gunpowder for the revolutionary armies

In memory of
....
.......departed this life
..... aged .. years &
.... days
She li... .... her dep...
...eth this monument ....
By her husband

(left and above) Charlotte W. Hoge Trollinger b. January 8, 1813 d. September 21, 1835 (22 years)

in 1776. He acquired 600 acres, and his son John Trollinger, acquired another 1,140 acres. John Trollinger Jr. inherited the property in 1840 after his father passed away. However, Charlotte did not benefit from the acquisition of land, which was known then as Pleasant Valley and later called Glen Mary. When giving birth to her third child, Charlotte died during labor. Her youngest daughter was honored by being named after her mother, Charlotte, and grandmother, Elizabeth (Howe) Hoge. Charlotte had been seven months pregnant when her grandmother had passed away; little did she know then how short her own life would be.

John Trollinger Jr. remarried in 1839 to Mary Grayson Wygal, the daughter of James Wygal and Mary Cecil. All were very prominent names in the Pulaski County area development since they were large landowners in Dublin. Formed in 1839, Pulaski County presented "a level of culture and quality of life" that was "generally improving." According to Mary Kegley, a prominent historian, it was "the highest type of rural civilization to be found in any part of Virginia's Great Southwest." These families mainly flourished due to the building of the Virginia-Tennessee Railroad. John Trollinger Jr. was given the prestigious position of the first agent of the railroad. His nomination was passed unanimously by the Board of Directors. His plantation was only half a mile away from the depot, and part of his land was "condemned" for the right-of-way with other large landowners. The railway benefited everyone in the area since goods for sale and other items could be transported the long distance to this former rural "shanty" town (as described by the future king of France when he visited).

Charlotte's daughter, Charlotte Elizabeth Trollinger, married Rev. John H. Hoge on March 18, 1856. He was a prominent Methodist minister and a physician, and this was his second marriage. Since he was Charlotte's cousin, they had the same great-grandfather, James Mayo Hoge. Her marriage, however, was short since she passed away on September 17, 1858, just shy of her 23rd birthday. Her husband remarried a year later to Sarah Trinkle, whose family, like the Trollingers, were devout Methodists and large landowners in Dublin.

Broken, weathered, and barely legible, much like her mother's gravestone, Charlotte Elizabeth Trollinger's marker is left woefully abandoned. Located in the Old Dublin Cemetery, also known as the Trollinger-Cecil-Trinkle Cemetery, she lies adjacent to her father, John Trollinger Jr., and her stepmother, Mary Grayson Wygal. She is buried among 826 souls, with the oldest grave being that of her grandfather, John Trollinger Sr., who died 18 years before her in 1840. Close by are two obelisks memorializing her husband, John. H. Hoge, and his third wife, Sarah. Although Charlotte is amongst the Trollinger family, she spends eternity away from her mother's grave at the Sunnyside Cemetery. Both mother and daughter died so very young with barely a trace of a memorial to remind us about their short time here on earth.

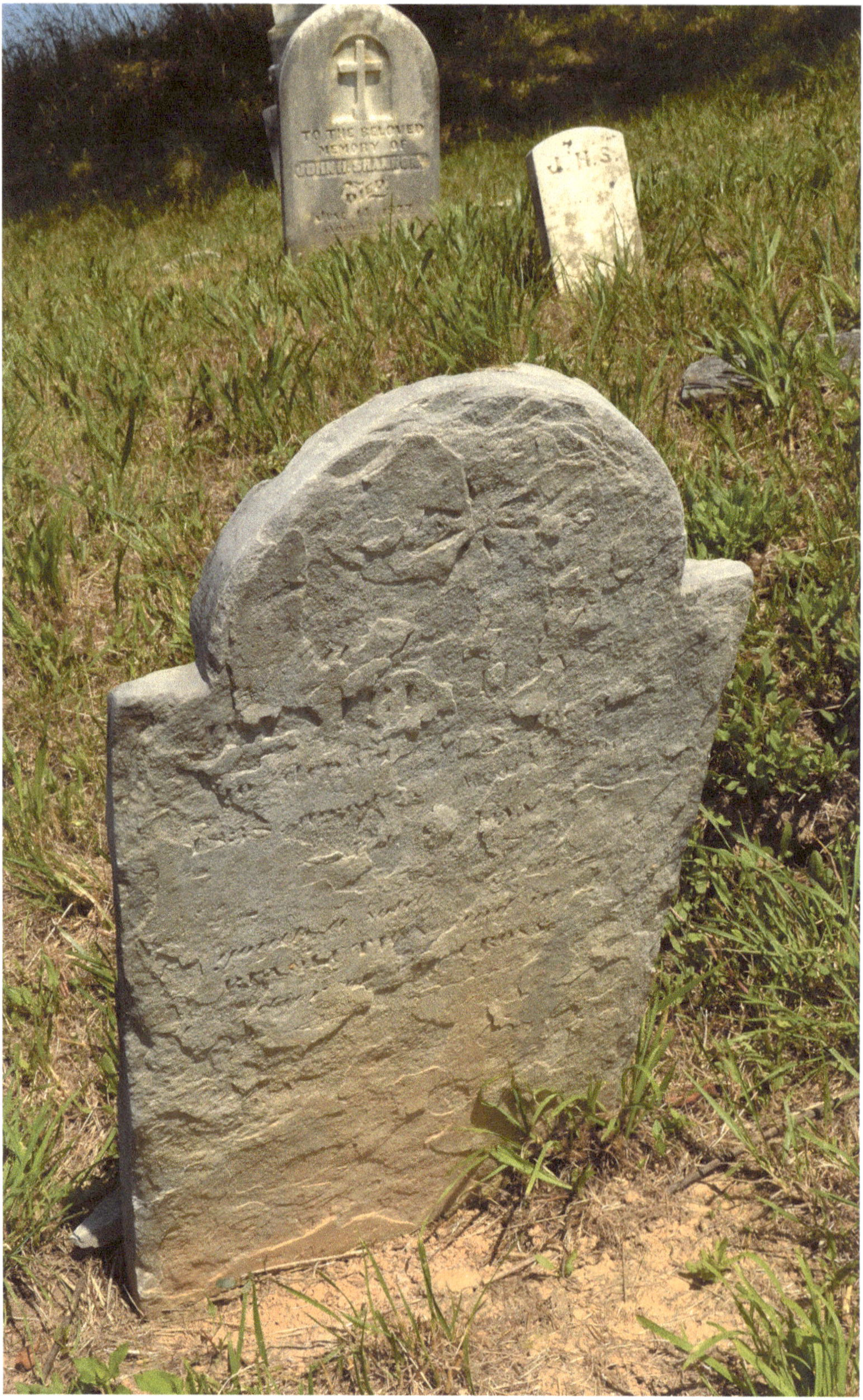
TO THE BELOVED
MEMORY OF
J. H. S.

CHAPTER 3

Romance in the Air

And now is he gone, how strange it seems.

But yesterday he moved as I.
But now his eye no longer beams
And low in dust he now must lie.
This voice which, spoke in kindest tones.
That showed the feelings of his heart.
That oft has soothed the sufferer's groans
Now with the body lies at rest.

> —Eliza Hoge about her grandfather, Major Daniel Howe, who departed on New Year's Eve 1838, she became Eliza Tyler in 1844.

ARRIVING IN THE NEW RIVER VALLEY'S WILDERNESS at only nine years old, Daniel experienced firsthand the harshness of the frontier. His father, Joseph, was a devout Presbyterian who emphasized virtue and duty. As he grew into manhood on his father's property, Sunnyside, a mental toughness ensued. At the young age of 18, he enlisted in the Continental Army in the Montgomery County Militia in 1776 during the Revolutionary War. Although it was initially for only a month, he returned in 1777 for a similar length of time. During this period, he did not engage in any battles but was responsible for guarding the frontier. In 1778, he became a captain, serving alongside Captain Preston and Captain Burke.

Nancy Heavin grew up in the New River Valley as the youngest daughter of Howard and Ruth Heavin (or Haven). The Heavins were originally from Scotland but emigrated to America due to religious persecution. Nancy's grandfather, John, began his new life in Maryland with his wife, Ruth. They gradually moved into the Southwest Virginia area, where they purchased 330 acres of land on the west bank of the new river, two miles south of Pepper's Ferry Rd, called Mount Lovely Tavern. It was there that Daniel and Nancy first met.

During the war, when Captain Howe was protecting the valley, he was ordered to observe the activities of known Tories in the country and arrest those who appeared to be a threat to the revolution. This stage of his military duty led to a romantic episode that profoundly impacted his life. The original story handed down from generation to generation is as follows:

> Dawn was breaking, and the welcomed rays of a cheerful May sun were pushing their way gently through the treetops along the hills to the east as Captain Daniel Howe mounted his horse and rode away from Sunnyside. A cavalry saber, primarily a badge of office, hung in a scabbard from his saddle. He was dressed in a coarse hunting shirt and buckskin breeches, the habitual attire of a militiaman of Colonial Virginia. The serious expression about his normally friendly blue eyes indicated that his mission was not a pleasant one. Inside his shirt was a warrant for the arrest of one Howard Haven, a Tory sympathizer, if not an avowed enemy of his country. On two previous occasions, the offender had escaped him. The third time he must not come away empty-handed.
>
> Topping the rise at the rim of the valley, the lone rider drew rein and leisurely turned to gaze back across the fertile farmlands. For a moment, his thoughts reverted to the past four years. Now a campaign-hardened veteran, he was only a lad in his teens, he mused, when in '76 he joined the military forces of his country and rode away to confront the dangers of the frontier. His mother had grieved to see him leave home at such an immature age. But, like all mothers, she could not accept that he was now old enough to take a man's part in the fight for independence; nor could she know what it meant to him to shoulder a musket and with frontiersmen like Burke, Taylor, McCorkle, Cloyd, and others share in the thrilling experiences

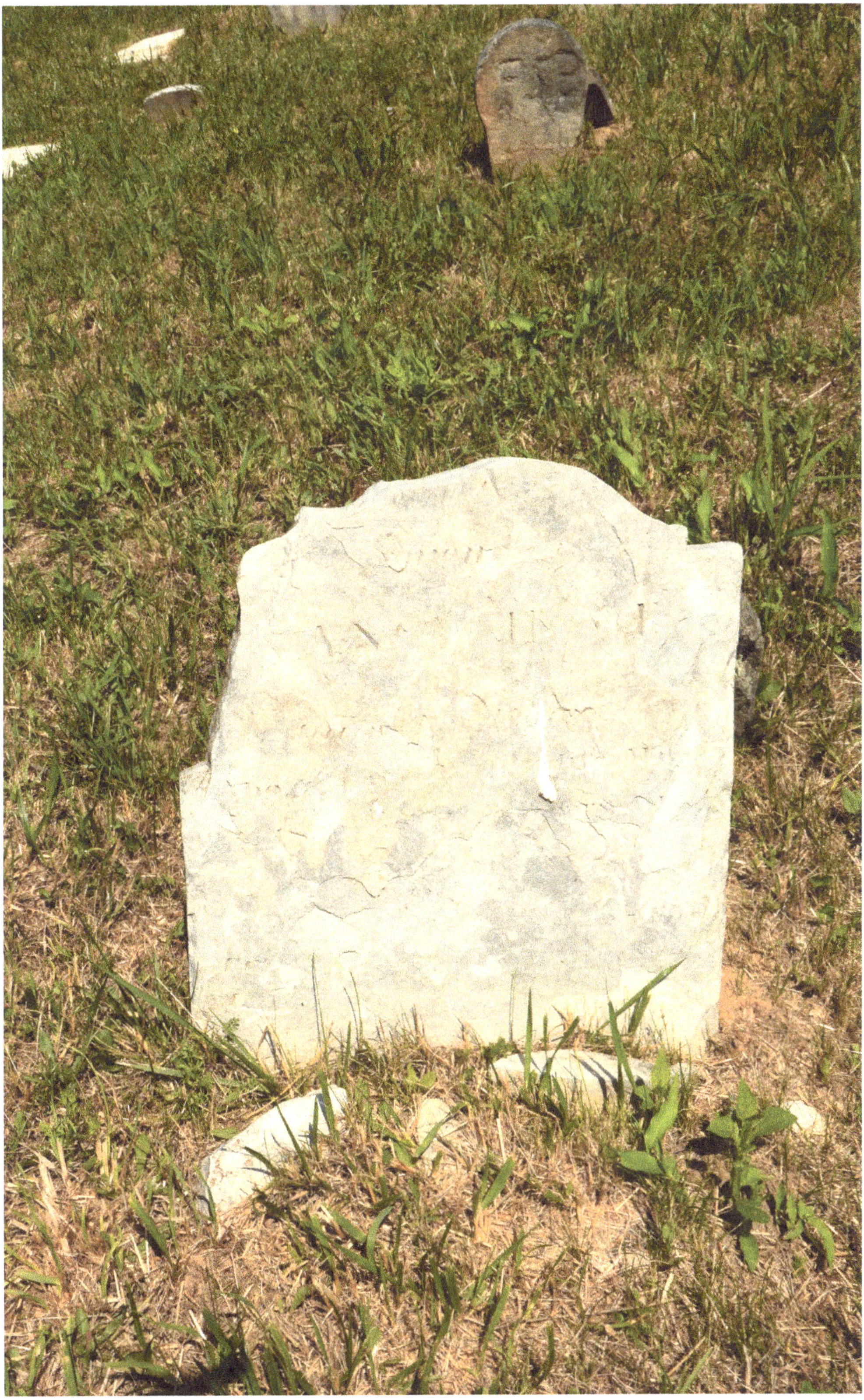

that far away places have to offer those of venturesome spirit. Now that these eventful years had passed, it seemed that fate had nothing in store for him but a humdrum life alone among the peaceful hills and green meadows of Back Creek. But after all, one can never tell what fate has to offer! Expanding his chest with a deep breath of the fresh morning air, he wheeled his horse about and set off over the forest road that led to Pepper's Ferry and the home of Howard Haven around the eastern bend of the river beyond.

The latter part of the morning, the lone horseman, Pepper's Ferry now several miles to his rear, was jogging along the river bottom road in deep thought when his meditations were interrupted by a young feminine voice softly singing "Barbara Allen." He was in front of the farm home of Howard Haven, and the voice was that of a little girl who sang with sweet and plaintive rhythm to the gentle gliding of a swing that hung from a limb of a large spreading apple tree in the front yard. He paused in admiration for a brief moment while she completed her song and brought the swing to a gradual stop.

To his salutation, she came to the gate and, with a friendly smile, said, "Won't you hitch your horse and come in?" As she unlatched the gate and stood there, her long, black curly locks and smiling brown eyes presenting a perfect picture of loveliness, she added, "I am Nancy Haven."

He gravely replied that he was Captain Daniel Howe, and when he explained that he had come to see her father on business of importance, her smile vanished. She suspected that his visit was not a friendly one, for she replied in no uncertain terms that her father and mother were both far from home and he need not wait for their return.

The captain suspected a prearranged plan to outwit the military authorities. He had met similar situations before, and he was not to be easily thwarted. After due deliberation, he expressed a desire to search the premises. To this proposal, little Nancy spiritedly replied, "Search to your heart's content. I have told you there is no one at home. I am sorry if you do not choose to take my word for it."

"Now are you satisfied?" she chided when the search was complete, and the only other human beings in evidence were found to be old "Uncle" Ben and "Aunt" Dinah. Still not a hint would she give of the whereabouts of her parents nor when she expected them to return.

Presently, Nancy grew friendly again, and the stern demeanor of her visitor was softened when she invited him to remain for the noonday meal, now being put on the table by the faithful colored servants. It was a wholesome meal of crisp fried chicken and gravy, cornbread and sweet potatoes, and while they partook of it, the little hostess listened with rapt attention to the captain's recital of some of the recent events. Hers was a small world. She had scarcely been beyond the limits of her farm home and those of the adjacent farm neighbors, the Peppers and the Shells. At last he arose to go, and when he thanked her for the excellent dinner and bade her goodbye, he added in a kindly voice, "Now, my little friend, you must not think hard of me, for after all a man in the service of his country must do his duty."

Her dark eyes flashed as she retorted, "And you must not think hard of my Daddy, either!" His heart was touched when her tone softened, and she added with a sweet smile, "But I'd like to have you come back again, anytime, for just a friendly visit."

He expressed his appreciation for her gracious manner and kindly thoughts towards one in his position, assuring her he would be most happy to return and renew their friendship after the end of the hostilities, which he hoped would be very soon. As he prepared to mount his horse, he added, "And by that time I feel sure our independence will be a reality, and with that issue settled, there will be no occasion to call on you armed like this and demand to search your home," concluding in a spirit of jest, "unless I have to do so to find you."

He flung himself lightly into the saddle and, with a cheerful farewell salute, rode away, his mission unaccomplished—and perhaps for the moment forgotten.

Thus, the story might end, except that there was a day of return. Future events led to the belief that Captain Daniel Howe did not go home that day entirely empty-handed. He carried with him the heart of a brown-eyed, spirited little Tory and left his own behind.

Sometime after the encounter, Daniel fought in the Battle of King's Mountain in the Carolinas. Although it only lasted 65 minutes, it was described as "the war's largest all-American fight" and a turning point in the revolution's eventual American victory. This battle undermined the British strategy in the South, and it became difficult for them to recruit American Loyalists to fight against the Patriots.

In the last year of his active service, Captain Daniel Howe, with the Montgomery County Militia, took part in General Greene's Guilford campaign of March 1781. When the British invaded Western North Carolina, the Montgomery County Militia and other available troops in the area were ordered south to assist General Greene in repelling the invader. The total force of 4,400 regulars and militiamen faced about 2,200 British. The American losses included 14 officers and 312 troops killed or wounded, but the British suffered more severely, leaving 93 dead in addition to the more than 500 wounded. The battle itself lasted only a few hours but resulted in a retreat from the Patriots to preserve the unit. The British declined to pursue them into the backcountry, leaving the British to acknowledge their failure to quash the South's resistance.

Later that year, the war ended, allowing Daniel to return to his home, Sunnyside. Continuing his service to the community, he became a gentlemen justice then a General Assembly member. Since the latter position required him to travel to Richmond, it allowed him to learn the day's news. This vital information contributed to his popularity in the New River Valley since there was no access to newspapers at the time. However, he had romantic interests to pursue as well.

Nancy and Daniel's courtship surfaced long after the first encounter during the war when she was just a child. The story continues . . .

> Some years later, one bright Sunday afternoon towards the end of summer, the same lone rider mounted his horse on Sunnyside's front lawn and set forth over the road that leads to Pepper's Ferry and the home of Howard Haven around the bend of the river beyond. From his immaculate attire and light-hearted manner, it was evident that this trip was not of a serious nature. War was long a thing of the past. The animosities and suspicions—the extreme feeling of colonist against Tory or loyalist—had been largely forgotten. The lone horseman, Daniel Howe, was now the master of Sunnyside and an industrious young gentleman farmer. Fate perhaps had much in store for him. He hummed the words of one of his favorite songs, "Barbara Allen," as he rode along with a light heart over the leaf-strewn forest trail. The birds in the trees overhead

appeared to join in the refrain. Romance was in the air.

The roadway around the bend of the river to the Haven farm home was now a well-beaten trail, so frequently had Daniel Howe made this trip during the past summer. Of the days of black curly locks and the apple tree swing, Nancy Haven had blossomed into beautiful womanhood. Theirs had been love at first sight and deep devotion at second. Daniel Howe and Nancy Haven sat under the same old spreading apple tree that night until a late hour. He held her hand while the silvery moon cast its shadows over the rippling waters of the nearby river. Soft words were spoken, and plans were made. There was nothing to mar the perfect serenity of this blissful summer evening together when they pledged never again to part.

They were married in August of 1790, just before Daniel's 33rd birthday; Nancy was 19 years old. Unfortunately, Nancy's father died three years before the nuptials. Her mother, Ruth, arranged for William, Nancy's eldest brother, to give her away at the family's farm home. A family celebration ensued, bringing the couple together from a romance that started long ago.

When his father died in 1794, Daniel inherited his cherished childhood home. Although he wasn't the oldest son, who customarily received the property, he was the oldest living in Virginia since his brother John moved to Kentucky. He busily engaged in developing and expanding the Sunnyside estate. Daniel increased his holdings to 1,200 acres of land along the Back Creek Valley. They raised cattle, flocks of sheep, and other livestock. They lived a happy and bountiful life raising 11 children on the estate, including Eleanor Haven Howe, General James Hoge's wife, but that was until a tragedy struck the family.

Nancy's mother, Ruth, disappeared for several months one spring. Her remains were later found in the tangled woods. It was presumed that her tragic death occurred when she became lost in the woods while on a trek to visit her grandchildren at Lovely Mount Tavern. An older woman at the time, 79 years old, Ruth was thought to have been carried into the woods by a bear or mountain lion that had attacked her. Ruth was a hearty frontier woman who typically followed Indian trails to save time, not the safest route. It must have been a horrific event for the youngest daughter, Nancy, to hear news about her mother, and she most likely did not want to discuss it with her young children. Her daughter Eleanor was only 16 years old, and the youngest, Nancy Pearis Howe, was only about

2. The fear and nightmares it would cause the children most likely kept the story silent for generations. However, the tale was kept alive in the papers of Mary Pepper Heavin, the wife of Ruth's son John, for us to tell.

Although the time is long past when the stately Major Daniel Howe first became smitten with the dark-eyed, spirited Nancy Heavin, they now rest in peace, side by side. Their stones are weather-worn from time and neglect, but the inscription is still preserved in writings: "In youth a soldier of the Revolution, in old age, a soldier of the cross," is inscribed on Daniel's stone along with a damaged symbol acknowledging his service.

Their three sons inherited the estate according to their will. Joseph, John, and William Howe became the stewards of Sunnyside. John bought out his brothers, eventually leaving the property to his daughter Agnes Shannon Howe. That is where Sunnyside's story comes to an end for the family and the beginning of the end of the cemetery's preservation.

JOHN ROGER
WAS
BORN
24TH OF
JUNE
1802
DIED
24TH OF
JUNE
1843

CHAPTER 4

Where the Weeping Willows Wave

How Soon In Dust He Lies Forgot

When love in solitude I stray
Reflecting on man's common lot
I think how frail is mortal clay
How soon in dust he lies forgot.

—Eliza Hoge (Tyler)
March 20, 1834

TIME PASSED WITHOUT ACKNOWLEDGMENT of a lost gravestone. With the marker covered, John Brawley Hoge did not receive any memorial wreaths honoring his life as a soldier, prosperous landowner, religious man, and family leader. In the overgrown, neglected cemetery, John's body, along with his elaborately carved headstone, lay covered with dirt. The stone lay broken until it was repaired a generation or so ago, although in vain. The elements, along with cattle and other animals, plowed over the marker, hiding it from the minimal visitors that passed by. Until one day, while trying to clean up the family cemetery, an edge of the stone peaked through the now short grass. Family members excitedly unearthed the stone, which clearly marked who he was and when he had

John Brawley Hoge b. Jun 24, 1772 d. Jun 24, 1847 (75 years)

died. Finally revealed, his stone tells the story of the man and his family that eternally rests beside him.

John was the son of James Mayo and Elizabeth Hoge; he was General James Hoge's older brother. At the end of the Revolutionary War, John was only 10 years old, too young to fight. Although it is uncertain when he enlisted in the navy, at 24 years old, he served in the 86th Regiment as an "ensign," which is the rank of the lowest commissioned officer. He became a lieutenant in Captain Maris's Company later that year. After the outbreak of the French Revolutionary War in 1793, America remained neutral toward the events that transpired between France and Great Britain, needing to build their own newly freed country. However, during this period until 1801, the British were aggressive, seizing American vessels and urging American citizens into service on behalf of the Royal Navy. It is uncertain which battles John may or may not have fought in, but he did serve his country, advancing into various leadership positions during those tumultuous years. We know he served in a different capacity in 1799, when he took up his father's post as commissioner of revenue.

Around 1799, John married his first wife, Prudence Montgomery, and had a daughter, Rachael Montgomery Hoge, born in early 1800. He then married Jane (Jenny) Rutledge in 1802 and had Eliza Ann and Jane Rutledge Hoge. We do not know precisely how John's first wives died; childbirth was the likely cause since it was precarious to have children in those days. Lastly, he married Elizabeth "Rippy" in 1807. They had seven children: Matilda, Rebecca Smith, Nancy Rippy, George Davies, Moses Howe, John Matthew Hoge (who would later earn the title of captain), and Margaret Reid Hoge.

John Hoge had large landholdings on Neck Creek close to Hayfield, where he grew up. It totaled over 1,012 acres, some of which he had bought from Thomas Cecil, including the White Glades track (south of Neck Creek). John only received $45 from his father, James Mayo Hoge, when he passed away in 1812. He received no land. His brother General James Hoge inherited the farm instead. The story goes that John used the money to buy his first piece of land, which included the historic log cabin built in 1800 on Neck Creek Rd. An unknown person built the house itself with only the initials "A.B." on the chimney giving any clue as to who the occupant was. Noted at his death in 1847, John acquired as much land as his brother the general, although it was not as well-watered as the Hayfield homestead. It sounds as though there may have been a little competition between the two Hoge brothers.

Unlike his brother, John was a very religious man. He was an elder in

In memory of
ELIZABETH HOGE
Born
Jan'y 12th 1782
Died
May 9th 185?

the New Dublin church until the abolitionists started to make the slave owners uncomfortable, which caused a divide. Believing in the "new school" ideology against slavery, he left with Rev. George Painter when they took a stand against enslavement. Forming a new congregation on his property called "White Glade" (now Belsprings), John became the elder of the newly formed presbytery. John's youngest daughter, Margaret, married Rev. William Hickman, who became the minister. Margaret received land from her father, two acres of which she gave to the church and the River View Presbyterian church for a joint cemetery. Since John was the only elder at the time, his death caused a significant loss for the congregation, as noted in their minutes following the memorial service:

> This church sustained a great loss by the death of Mr. John Hoge, which took place Jun 24, 1847. Mr. Hoge had for many years been a ruling elder in New Dublin and at the time of his death was the only elder in White Glade church. His last illness was short, but very painful, which he bore with great patience and Christian resignation. Death was disarmed. His end was peace. He died on his birthday, aged 75 Blessed are the dead which die in the Lord.

John Hoge's inventory the year he died lists the following:

> 8 slaves (4 men, one old woman, two boys, and a girl) and household furniture including two looking glasses, two clocks, a desk, a dining table, a secretary and bookcases with books, four beds and furniture, as well as 14 horses, 21 steers plus other assorted cattle and hogs, and sheep, which with the kitchen and barn equipment and other goods came to a total value of $4,477.75." The value of his estate would have been about $140,000 in today's dollar.

In his will, he left the farm that he lived on to his youngest son, Captain John Matthew Hoge, who would receive two-thirds of it when his father passed and the other third when his mother, Elizabeth, died. He helped his oldest son, George, to establish a mercantile business by giving him $3,000 in 1837 before he died and confirming this in his will. Moses, the middle son, inherited the land on the New River called the Still Water Tract. He left his youngest daughter, Margaret Reid Hoge Hickman, the White Glade tract adjoining the home place, Sunnyside. Previously made advancements to some daughters are noted in the will since they were all to be made equal. John also mentioned his children from his two

Charlie Hoge b. Jan 22, 1846 d. Jun 8, 1847 (1 year)

Elizabeth M. Hoge b. Jan 14, 1851 d. Feb 14, 1854 (3 years)

prior marriages and left their children, his grandchildren, an inheritance instead of his first children directly. Elizabeth Rippy Hoge died a couple of years after her husband and rests by his side. Curiously, she amended her will one month before her death to include the children from her husband's first marriage. She was then able to rest in peace.

To signify Elizabeth's ability to lie in peace, her tombstone is adorned with a bed, representing rest. Also included on her stone, a willow tree sits prominently between the bed and an urn. Although willow trees are associated with grief, they also represent immortality. A willow tree will flourish and remain whole no matter how many branches someone might cut off—possibly a metaphor for their family tree. An urn that generally represents mourning often accompanies the willow tree on gravestones from this era. As Elizabeth's life on earth came to an end, although their family was in mourning, her son John's story was just beginning.

Before Captain John Matthew Hoge moved into his father's home on Neck Creek, he had a baby boy with his first wife, Mary Black, named Charlie. This little boy was only a year and a half old when he died just a couple of weeks before his grandfather John Hoge. This lost soul was only discovered in 2018 when his gravestone was unearthed after being hidden for generations. Unlike his grandfather, Charlie was not in the family's records. The short life of this tiny child was unknown for so many years.

Charlie's sister, Elizabeth M. Hoge, was born before her grandmother, also named Elizabeth, passed away. She was able to enjoy the farm of her ancestors for only a short time. Only three years old when she died, her birth and death went unrecorded except on her gravestone, which was hiding in plain sight under overgrown weeds in the family cemetery. Her headstone, adorned with flower buds, symbolic of the renewal of life, beautifully shines in the sun. These two precious children were laid to rest next to their grandparents for eternity. These two untold souls can now be added to their family tree with their siblings, Nanci (Nannie), Lucy, Rhoda, and Jennie Hoge, and their descendants.

On Elizabeth's tombstone the inscription reads, "Short pain - - - short grief - dear babe, was thine, Now joys eternal and divine," from *Solace for Bereaved Parents*.

> Sweet babe no more, but seraph now
> Before the throne, behold her bow;
> To heavenly joys her spirit flies,
> Blest in the triumph of the skies;
> Adores the grace that brought her there

Without a wish—without a care;
That wash'd her soul in Calv'ry's stream,
That shorten'd life's distressing dream.
Short pain - - - short grief - dear babe, was thine,
Now joys eternal and divine,

Yes, thou art fled, and saints a welcome sing,
Thine infant spirit soars on angels' wing;
Our dark affection would have hop'd thy stay,
The voice of God has call'd His child away.
Like Samuel, early in the temple found,
Sweet Rose of Sharon, plant of holy ground;
Oh! more than Samuel blest, to thee 'tis given,
The God he serv'd on earth, to serve in Heaven.

Captain John suffered more loss when his wife passed away after more than 25 years of marriage. Interestingly, he went on to marry Mary T. Hoge, who was about 20 years younger. But more notably, they had the same great-grandfather, James Hoge Sr., although different great-grand-mothers. Mary was also the sister of Moses and Achilles Hoge, who both lost their lives in The Battle of Cloyd's Mountain, famously documented in the book *My Two, My Only Sons*. John and Mary both suffered signifi-cant losses in each of their lives, which might have brought them closer together. They shared the same family history, with similar sadness and joys, and lived happily together on their property for almost 20 years.

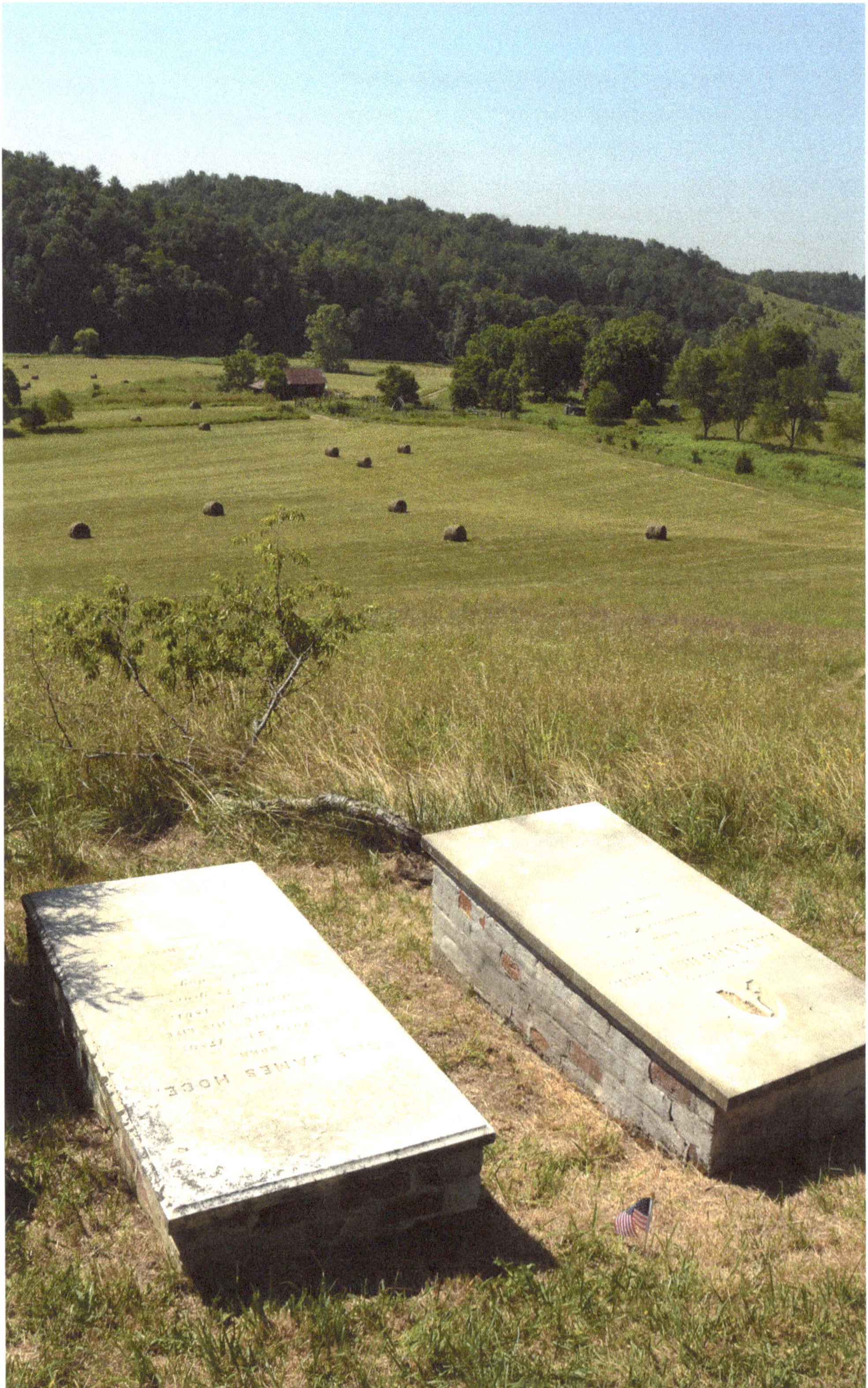

CHAPTER 5

Tis Only Noble to Be Good

We Live in Deeds, Not Years

We live in deeds, not years; in thoughts, not breaths;
In feelings, not in figures on a dial.
We should count time by heart-throbs. He most lives
Who thinks most, feels the noblest, acts the best.
And he whose heart beats quickest lives the longest:
Lives in one hour more than in years do some
Whose fat blood sleeps as it slips along their veins.
Life's but a means unto an end; that end,
Beginning, mean, and end to all things—God.
The dead have all the glory of the world.

—Philip James Bailey, 1884, quoted in the
Wake Forest Law Review, October 1972,
In Appreciation of James Fulton Hoge, Jr.

BY THE SIDE OF HIS FIRST COUSIN AND LOVING WIFE, Eleanor, General James Hoge rests in peace among his ancestors and descendants. The etching on his large tomb is a simple statement, "To Our Father." Only two tombs sit prominently among the gravestones in the Sunnyside Cemetery: one for General James Hoge and a matching one for Eleanor, who passed suddenly five years prior to him from an apparent heart attack, noted by Governor J. Hoge Tyler in his diary. A broken column, symbolizing dying

General and Eleanor Hoge's tombs

before old age, adorns her tomb. She was 63. As stated on top of her grave, the inscription proclaims her life well lived, but a sudden loss:

> Her pious and useful life was extended to an honorable old age and closed by a sudden death. Her charity had its source in religion. Her love for her neighbor was the genuine effect of her love for God. Her resignation was the fruit of her faith, and she died in Hope because she had lived A Christian.

The year was 1856, and the Republican Party had just been formed. A few years earlier, some Wisconsin citizens met in a schoolhouse to support the abolition of slavery. This early group adopted "Republicans" as their name, and this first meeting and subsequent activities would lead to the eventual election of Abraham Lincoln. *Uncle Tom's Cabin*, published about this time, profoundly affected people's attitude toward slavery, which set the groundwork for this abolitionist movement and the Civil War.

Hotly debated slavery issues continued to occur while Eleanor laid to rest. Proslavery groups in Kansas attacked the free-soil town of Lawrence earlier in the year and radical abolitionist John Brown and his followers continued to strike in retaliation until he was tried and convicted of treason in 1859. But Eleanor rested in peace during the political violence in Virginia. She now enjoys Sunnyside's eternal view, where her parents, Major Daniel Howe and Nancy Heavin, raised her and her ten siblings. Her grandson, Gov. James Hoge Tyler, described her as follows:

> In Mrs. Howe's veins flowed some of the proudest English blood, but her ancestor had thrown away his title to the trappings of heraldry to espouse the cause of liberty, so she ever impressed on this boy that.
>
> Tis only noble to be good,
>
> Kind hearts are more than coronets,
>
> And simple faith than Norman blood.

Before we delve into Eleanor's life, we must first introduce her husband, General James Hoge, who was 10 years older. He grew up alongside the neighboring family, the Howes. His parents were Elizabeth Howe and James Mayo Hoge. Elizabeth's family built Sunnyside. James Mayo Hoge built a cabin they called Hayfield, which was within sight of the Howe residence. James Hoge and his 10 siblings shared the small dwelling made from plainly hewn logs situated in dense wilderness. Afraid to venture far from the cabin in fear of being attacked by Indians, the young James had ample time for his chores.

At the turn of the nineteenth century, peace and tranquility became the norm as the population increased; however, it was still sparse there compared to Northern Virginia. Since there were no modern conveniences, life on the farm was hard. Work was from sunup until sundown with there always being something to do on the expansive property. After their long day of chores, the family would tell tales of the early settlers, Indian raids, or the American Revolution. On other nights in their small log cabin lit by candlelight, they read the bible or learned the three Rs.

The property had a mill that did the grinding for the neighborhood. It stood where the dam on Belle-Hampton is now. An Indian once shot some family members off of the fence near where the general store currently stands. Another Indian died at the mouth of Shuffle Branch, where it empties into Back Creek. The poor Indian was shot near the mill and waded down to the creek to prevent blood from being traced. The wound had grass stuffed inside to try to stop the blood, but to no avail. With these incidents, it is not surprising that James was extremely afraid to go through the woods to the gristmill in fear of being captured. In those days, the Indians had a town in what is now a field across the creek. Although James grew up during peak slavery in America, the Indians were the main topic of discussion. The massacre at Draper's Meadows in 1755 still sent chills down the spines of the people across the valley.

As a youngster, James lived an impoverished life, so he contributed to the family as much as he could. Mauling, or splitting rails, earned him a sense of perseverance and the strength of an ox. Old tales assert that the first horse James owned, he rode to Big Sandy, then part of Montgomery County, where it proceeded to die. He then was seen walking back home carrying his saddle and bridle with him, approximately 85 miles. He went on to become a senior magistrate who had a sheriff's role in Montgomery County. These experiences led to a life of service and his successful military career.

Since General James Hoge was 10 years older than Eleanor, the pair's romance story came later. After being away, James returned to Hayfield to find the young Eleanor in tears on his family's cabin steps. When he inquired as to what caused her sadness, she confided that her parents wanted her to marry someone she did not love. Comforting her with a gentle hug, James assured her the predicament would be solved. When she questioned his definitiveness, he declared his long-time deep love for her, which he had kept to himself until now, and he pledged to marry her.

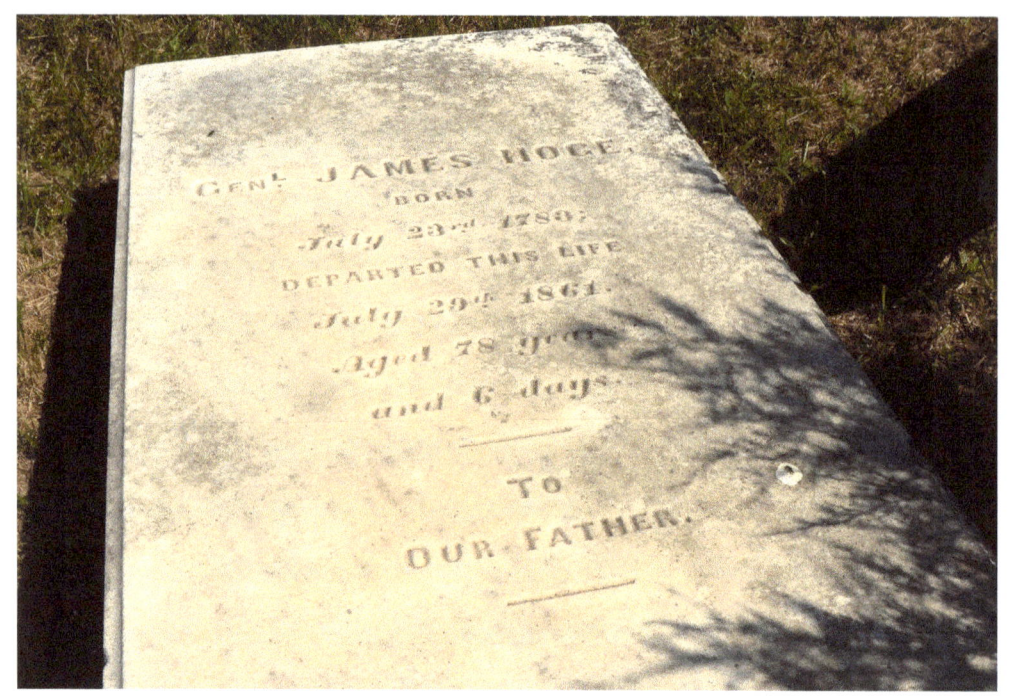

General James Hoge b. Jul 23, 1783 d. Jul 29, 1861 (78 years)

Feeling mutual about her cousin, Eleanor agreed to the proposal—problem solved. They enjoyed a long and happy life together on the property he inherited several years later.

In the first half of the 1800s, Virginia supposedly experienced an agricultural depression due to the lack of useful farming techniques such as crop rotation, causing the thriving land to fail. People were bound for the west because of the opportunities there for a better living. While others moved west, Eleanor and the general lived an extraordinary life on a piece of rich, rolling countryside with bountiful clear springs where they raised four boys, Daniel Howe, James Fulton, Joseph Haven, and William Edward, and one daughter, Eliza. Dutifully, Eleanor stayed with the young Daniel when he was only three years old along with servants and farmhands while James fought in the War of 1812 as a captain. He left Christiansburg for Norfolk in April of 1814 as commander of the Montgomery formed company. While stationed in Norfolk, an oppressive fever erupted, causing half of his men to either become sick or die. When he returned home after the United States and Britain signed the Treaty of Ghent to end the war, Eleanor became pregnant with Eliza, who was born in December of 1815.

After having five children and living in the small log cabin, James decided to build a stunning brick home to raise their growing family. Made

Eleanor Haven Howe b. Dec 1, 1792 d. Jun 13, 1856 (63 years)

by master builder John Swope, a Hessian, the general's two-story home incorporated six window bays in a Flemish bond facade. Created by a farmhand with a penknife, the most elaborate Federal-style wooden mantel with decorative detail adorned their dining room fireplace. A honing tool was found during 2020 renovations, strategically laid in the dining room window sash, most likely from a farmhand that helped construct the house. He was probably letting us know he was there—like an artist's signature. Although the structure's brick descended two feet deep to keep the home safe from intruders, embellished custom wood trim and floors made from heart pine were installed to reflect the owners' status.

In addition to the "mansion house," there were numerous outbuildings. A cooking and laundry cottage was built, equipped with indoor and outdoor wood-burning cookstoves. Located steps away from the kitchen was an expansive brick smokehouse for curing meat. The nearby spring accommodated a substantial stone springhouse where milk and butter were kept cool. James inherited from his father the gristmill that ground their grain into flour on nearby Back Creek. On Belle Hampton Rd, he built a brick blacksmith structure with a forge chimney by Shuffle Branch Creek. Erected about 1850 was a bank barn used for horses and their prized cattle. Finally, a farm store was also probably built during this period, eventually including a post office in the late 1800s.

Serving as a "gentlemen justice" in Montgomery County, James and 15 other magistrates were assigned to conduct court proceedings during each quarter. Some of their duties consisted of laying and disbursing tax levies; licensing taverns and ferries; appointing road viewers; and appointing county officials, such as court officers, school commissioners, constables, deputies, overseers of the poor, road surveyors, and other commissioners. The justices, who were mainly farmers, were selected by their reasoning ability and common sense. This position was one of service which didn't receive pay. Despite their immense power, they served the county well and were considered the county's "Fathers." Noted for their law-abiding character, the people in the area didn't cause trouble, which allowed the justices to maintain peace successfully.

In 1839, the citizens of the western part of Montgomery, where James lived, and eastern part of Wythe county petitioned Virginia's General Assembly to create a new county. It was named Pulaski county after Count Casimir Pulaski, an exiled Polish nobleman. During the American Revolution, he had fought bravely as part of George Washington's army but was fatally wounded at Savannah in 1779. As a county seat location, they chose Newbern, the only village in the newly formed county. It was an ideal location since it was located in the center and on a stagecoach road. James was one of these first county fathers as well as his brother John. There were seven schools listed in 1840 as primary and common schools accommodating 136 students in one-room log schoolhouses. The county was known for its rich bluegrass land, which raised some of the country's finest cattle. There were seven gristmills, five sawmills, and ten stores operating in the county. In 1840, when the census came out a year after the county was established, the list of families inventoried were considered "First Families of Pulaski County," or FFPC for short.

Although he started life underprivileged, the general amassed a considerable fortune of a quarter of a million dollars and accumulated approximately 8,000 acres of pristine countryside, which he left to his children and grandson. Collecting the acreage from other Virginians who possibly were departing for the west, the general managed his estate wisely. He raised prized cattle on land with an abundance of fresh spring water, rolling terrain for exercise, and a climate exempt from extremes. But it was the land he owned with a foundation of limestone that could produce rich, inexhaustible sod for the "finest bluegrass unsurpassed anywhere in the world." These were considered ideal conditions for quality cattle. He installed fencing on almost 2,000 acres to protect his investment. The general's operation also included crops. Taking advantage of the fast-growing plant hemp, he sold a large supply to the shipping industry, which used it for rope. As a self-taught businessman, the general left a rich legacy to his descendants and his community, reflected in his lifetime of service.

The general was a leader amongst men. His charge was "Enter life free from prejudice; form your own opinions, and do not attach too much importance to statements made by those who allow prejudice to bias their judgment," and "go security for no man." Magnificent in appearance, he had piercing and merry black eyes and prominent brows. He was always wearing brilliant uniforms and riding the finest horses, characteristics of a classic Virginia gentleman. Admirers, it was said, would gather around to hear him speak, for which he had a talent. His intellect was strong, and his resolve for integrity noticeable by neighbors and countrymen.

Eleanor, known as a devote Christian, contrasted with the general, who did not find religion until nearly sixty. He never approached or raised the subject until, one day, his wife summoned her sister Luenma, her daughter Eliza, and niece Rebecca. They assembled in a private room at Sunnyside when the general had left for business in Newbern. He would be gone all day, and Eleanor bound the girls to secrecy not to mention their meeting to anyone. She proposed that the group pray for the general's conversion and read the bible for several hours. But a little while in, a servant's announcement interrupted their devotions. The general had returned early. This frightened his wife, who assumed something was terribly wrong. But after he dismounted his horse, he quietly took Eleanor's arm, leading her into the garden. There, he told her that "firm conviction" had come upon him on the ride to Newbern, causing him to return to tell her he wanted to join the church.

The first church Eleanor belonged to was New Dublin, but there grew a rift between members in the early 1830s. The abolitionists became vocal and antislavery unrest made slave owners uncomfortable. Some of the "new school" members left the church and attended Page's Meetinghouse, but they were a separate unit within the congregation. In 1843, they resolved to form a new presbytery, and when missionaries arrived, their plan became a reality with the formation of "White Glade" (now named Belsprings) in Pulaski County. Among the first seventeen members were Eleanor and her daughter. Rev. William Hickman, who married Margaret Hoge, the general's niece, became the pastor. Although we suspect the group continued initially to share the Page's Meetinghouse for services, we don't know for sure since they may have congregated in people's homes instead. Eliza was most likely married by Rev. Hickman in 1844, which also coincides with the time the general decided to attend church. A brick church was established in 1850 near the growing community of Bell Spring. Eventually, they decided to change their name after the town it resided in, Belspring.

Sadly, in his last seven years, the general was paralyzed and could barely get around, leaving his 10-year-old grandson, J. Hoge Tyler, to manage the farm. Young Hoge enjoyed riding around on his pony named Moley, but under the general's directions, he would attend to the farm's business. Fortunately, he also had an overseer named William Echols and his family to help. After the first great battle of Manassas in the Civil War, also known as the Battle of Bull Run, General James Hoge left the world to be with his wife and daughter for eternity. Besides his paralysis, he struggled with gravel, now known as kidney stones. His last words were a prayer for his grandson, J. Hoge Tyler, the heir to the Hayfield estate.

Annually the grass grows high above the tombs, covering their location from outsiders. At one time, cattle meandered into the cemetery causing damage to many graves; however, Eleanor and James's tombs stand strong, only worn by the elements and time. The cemetery is no longer forgotten by the family and receives yearly maintenance to uncover and even discover more souls buried there. A tradition honoring soldiers who served our country, an American flag is placed at their graves every July 4.

WILLIAM

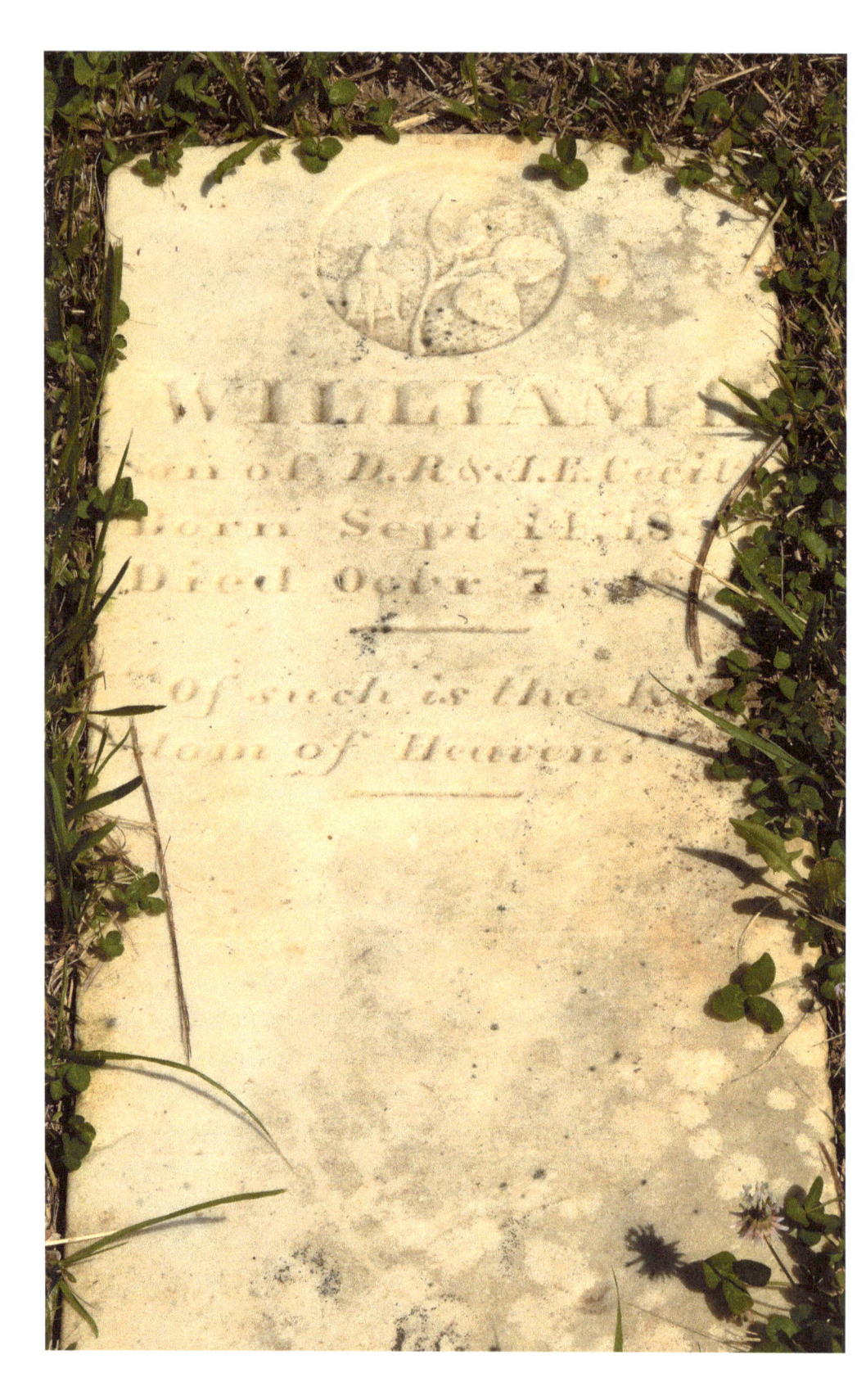

Son of D. R. & J. E. Cecil

Born Sept 11, 18

Died Oct'r 7

"Of such is the Kingdom of Heaven"

CHAPTER 6

Let the Little Children Come to Me

On the Death of an Infant

Thy race of life so soon hath past
That scarce we knew that thou wert here
E'er death had snatched thee from our grasp
We heeding all our cries and tears
Yes lovely infant, ere thou knew
The wretched world that thou was in
Thy spirit to the savior flew
Where yet thy hear knew not to sin
Now in the blessed arms of him
Who once to little children said.

Suffer these little lambs to come
For them my precious blood was shed
There in my Father's Kingdom shine
Forever bright; and in his praise
These little tongues which are divine
In endless Hallelujah raise.

—Eliza Hoge (Tyler), March 20, 1834

William H. Cecil b. Sept. 14, 1850 d. Oct. 7, 1850 (1 month)

ENGRAVED WITH ROSEBUDS, symbolizing the fragile beginning of a life that was cut short, the Cecil children's gravestones lay with Major Daniel Howe's (1758–1838) grandchildren and great-grandchildren. They are not the oldest graves in the family cemetery; however, they did precede their great-grandparents. Although toppled over, William Cecil's gravestone is the only record of his short life on earth. The monument has been washed clean from the sun, and a recognizable message is etched across the stone, "of such is the kingdom of heaven." This extract is taken from the book of Matthew 19:14: "But Jesus said, 'Let the little children come to Me, and do not forbid them; for of such is the kingdom of heaven.'"

Julia Ann's gravestone, however, is worn and discolored by the elements. It stands strong amongst its knocked over neighbors. The words are barely legible, but after careful deciphering, a quote from "Death of a Young Child" in *Psalms and Hymns* becomes clear:

> Alas! How changed that lovely flower
> Which bloomed and cheered my heart
> Fair, fleeting comfort of an hour,
> How soon we're called to part.

William and Julia Ann were two of Daniel Rufus Cecil (1824–1906) and Ardelia Pearis Cecil's (1825–1873) seven children. Daniel and Ardelia were both in their early twenties when they wed in 1848 and were both related to the Howe family. As first cousins, now spouses, they would have spent much of their time exploring Sunnyside in their youth. The Hoges routinely spent family celebrations and festivities together with the Howes since their histories were intertwined.

The Cecil family were among the original settlers in Dublin when they arrived in 1768, along with the Cloyds, Wygals, Millers, and Trollingers. Samuel Cecil (1719–1786) and his family, considered Maryland aristocrats, built a mansion three miles northeast of town at the beginning of Neck Creek, encompassing 1,000 acres. Samuel served in the Revolutionary War under the command of Capt. Cloyd. His grandson Zachariah White Cecil (1798–1870) married Julia Howe (1795–1865), Major Daniel Howe and Elizabeth Haven Howe's daughter, in 1814. Their son, Daniel Rufus Cecil, was born 10 years later.

The Pearis family initially resided in Montgomery County when they moved to Southwest Virginia, but later moved to Giles County, VA, where they founded Pearisburg. Captain George Pearis (1745–1782) married El-eanor Haven Howe (1755–1780) in 1771. Captain Pearis was a Revolutionary War captain in the militia. He injured his shoulder in

JULIA ANN

daughter of D.R. & J.E. Cecils
Born Feby 15th 1852
Died Feby 15th 1854

the Battle of Shallow Ford in North Carolina, returning home wounded and disabled from further service. His wife passed away just a few days after his homecoming. Although heartbroken from his loss and circumstance, he moved to Giles County, where he later donated land for the town's founding. Eleanor, who was only 25 years old when she died (and the oldest grave in the county), left a lasting legacy with her nine children. Her oldest son, Colonel George Neeley Pearis Jr., married his first cousin, Elizabeth Haven Howe (1791–1862), in 1808. They had seven children, one of them named Ardelia Eleanor Pearis.

Now returning to Daniel and Ardelia's story, the married couple started raising their family in Pulaski County, Virginia. As a farming family, they benefited from this bountiful Garden of Eden. The land was generous with plenty of water and wildlife. Bears and deer could provide food and hides. Plentiful trees supplied them with a source of heat as well as materials to build cabins. But there was still plenty of labor required to work the land which provided for the family. Daniel's mother, Julia, came to live with them shortly after their marriage, most likely to help with the children. They eventually moved to Giles County, where their family continued to grow. At this point, they had the resources for more laborers to help, although Julia stayed with them until she died in 1865.

As the war ended, no longer was Daniel's mother around to help. Nor were the seven laborers freed that same year; the Cecils struggled with the reconstruction of their farm. The Panic of 1873, a depression for the country, triggered several traumatic years for the Cecils and coincided with the unfortunate and untimely death of Ardelia at 47 years old. These events left the young family in disarray during the reconstruction of the South. Daniel only had his two sons, aged 17 and 13, to help on his homestead, Walkers Creek, in Pearisburg. He later remarried Sophia Anderson (1834–1912) in 1886, and they happily lived together on the farm for 20 more years until his death in 1906.

The Cecil family cemetery located in Prospectdale, Giles County, has 14 graves. The cemetery originated with the death of Julia Howe Cecil. It also serves as the resting place of Daniel Rufus Cecil and his wives, Ardelia and Sophia. One daughter, Elizabeth Pearis Cecil Eaton, who lost her husband, James C. Eaton (1850–1882), fifty years before her own passing in 1932, is memorialized in the graveyard. But over 10 years prior to her passing, graves of the babes were abandoned and left behind when Sunnyside, including the cemetery, was sold outside of the family.

William and Julia Ann Cecil's tiny plots lay alone in Pulaski County among prominent family members. Their small graves are overshadowed by the long list of war heroes from the French and Indian War, the Revolutionary War, the War of 1812, and the Civil War. Hidden for decades amongst the weeds in the vast pastures of Sunnyside, they have barely survived the elements. Though their life was brief, their ancestral legacy is now recorded for future generations.

AGNES S.
Daughter of
A. H. &
E. G. DeJARNETTE
DIED
JAN. 15,

CHAPTER 7

Our Little Ones

Childhood

There's many a pain, and many a joy,
In the life of every girl and boy;
There's many a smile, and many a tear,
Many a sorrow, for mother to cheer.

There's many a foe and many a friend,
Many a toy, to borrow and lend;
A cloud will come, and then it's flown.
Anger has gone, love stays alone.

—Lily Tyler, daughter of Gov. James Hoge Tyler
February 26, 1896

LITTLE AGNES'S GRAVE SITS LOVINGLY next to that of her grandfather, Major John Dunbar Howe. She died six days after her grandfather passed away. She was only two years old. A lamb adorns her gravestone, symbolizing the innocence of dying so young. Her inscription reads, "The only path she trod was that which leads from the mother's arms into the arms of God." Little Agnes was the oldest daughter of Agnes Shannon Howe and Eugene Grant De Jarnette. Her older brother, John, was four years old, and her baby sister, Sara, was four months old when Agnes died.

Agnes's mother, Agnes Shannon Howe, was born and grew up on Sunnyside, which she inherited in 1885. She took care of her father during his "inactive" years of life. In 1881, her oldest son, John, was born at Sunnyside, so we know the family lived there at least by that time. John was named after his grandfather and spent four blissful years communing with nature in the beautiful valley among the fruit trees, the vineyards, the lush forest, and babbling creek. Living in bliss on his family's ancestral homestead didn't prepare him for the burden of death in the family.

Siblings so close in age typically have a close bond, making it an even greater tragedy for the family. Young children are often confused by death, which causes fear, anxiety, and guilt. At the very least, it is a loss of innocence. Young John's grandfather and sister dying so close in time undoubtedly confused him. To a child so youthful, the grief of so many people surrounding him must have been puzzling. Having someone explain to him that his sister is in heaven and that God is listening would have nonetheless been reassuring.

OUR LITTLE ONES

God Will Hear
by Lily Tyler

God will hear you, little one,
Whensoe'er you pray,
At the dreary midnight hour,
And the busy day.

God will hear you, when you say
"Now I lay me down to sleep";
If in faith you ask his help,
He, his little one will keep.

God will hear you, little one,
He is always near;
If you truly trust His love,
You need never fear.

The De Jarnette family continued living their life on the farm through the heartbreaks. A daughter was born the next year, Caroline, who indeed brought joy to the grieving family. Known as Callie, she could relish the pleasures of innocence and the bountiful beauty of her surroundings. Five years passed before another sibling, Margaret, came into the world.

Sara, Caroline, Margaret, and John spent their childhood in the valley, but that came to an end in 1901. The De Jarnette family sold the old home place, relinquishing it from the family legacy after 143 years. Little Agnes's grave was left behind in the cemetery next to her grandfather, and as the family moved to Richmond, VA, the Howe/Hoge Cemetery began its demise. No longer owned by the family, little maintenance or access to the 28 graves started their incomprehensible decline. Since they were exposed to the elements, the gravestones deteriorated or broke. The graves themselves became swallowed up by the grasses, which grew unforgivingly for generations.

But while Agnes sleeps, the cemetery is experiencing a revitalization. The mission of family members now is to uncover the lives of the residents and celebrate those buried here. Although not yet in the family's possession, access and care are abound. Regular clean-up and soon repairs will honor those who have lived exemplary lives and will be remembered for generations to come.

NELLIE

Daughter of
J. MOORE & SUE H. TYLER
Born Aug. 28, 1890
Died April 15, 1893

CHAPTER 8

Not My Will But Thine Be Done

> Yet surely should the parent's voice be welcome to the child
> Whether it come at noon or night,—in gentle tones or wild;
> And I, oh Father! When Thy will shall call my soul away
> May I as calmly hear Thy word,—as placidly obey!
>
> —*Passion Flowers: Ashes of Roses,* 1854
> By Julia Ward Howe (of no known relationship)

NELLIE'S FATHER, JAMES "HOGE" TYLER, WAS THE GRANDSON of General James Hoge. The general's only daughter, Eliza, died just hours after giving birth to her son, who they called Hoge. This tale begins with a young Hoge being carried in a champagne basket back to Hayfield Farm in a carriage alongside his grandmother, Eleanor Hoge, and a nursemaid, Sara Armstead. Raised by his grandparents, he was well educated and taught the business of farming. Sara, who he called Auntie, nursed him and helped raise him as her own. He had his grandparents' heartstrings. They often spoiled him, but although he received a pony named Moley at 10 years old, it was necessary to help his grandfather manage the property. The general, paralyzed at the time, could not care for his large estate anymore. Hoge would roam the farm on Moley, overseeing the workers until his grandfather's death, which just so happened to coincide with the start of the Civil War.

With no mother or grandparents to raise him, Hoge moved in with his father, George Tyler. His father was married to his fourth wife at that time and was now responsible for a number of children. Hoge was promptly sent away to a private school to continue his education. At the academy, there were stories and imaginations of the adventures of war, and Hoge and his friends wanted to experience the battles themselves. Not to be separated from his friends, he joined as a private in the Confederate Army instead of an officer once he turned 16 years old. He served for two years until Lee surrendered to Grant at Appomattox.

Shortly after the Confederate defeat in May of 1865, while Hoge visited Christiansburg, he met Sue Montgomery Hammet. He fell in love with her at first sight. After being acquainted with her for only five short months, he proposed at a tournament in Christiansburg, where he crowned her "Queen of Love and Beauty." Married in 1868, they lived happily on the family farm, Hayfield. Since the war left the property with a dismantled home and unfenced and worn fields stripped of any vegetation, they spent their time rebuilding. Along with starting the finest heard of Durham cows, they brought the farm back to its original grandeur. Their first son, Edward, was born a year after their marriage, in 1869, followed by James Hoge Jr., Stockton Heth, Belle Norwood, Sue Hampton, Henry Clement, Eliza, and Eleanor (Nellie) Howe.

Before the youngest girls were born, Hoge renovated the home of his grandfather. He built a front porch with octagonal pillars in the fashionable Italianate style, a two-story foyer, grand staircase, front foyer, upstairs hall, and front bedroom in 1879. Hoge renamed the home Belle-Hampton after his daughters Belle and Sue Hampton. During this period, Hoge opened a coal operation on his land, which he called Belle-Hampton Coal Mine. Since his mine was so successful, he went on to build a general store/post office, which sold tobacco, cotton from the farm, and other staples to accommodate his workers. So numerous were the miners' families, they formed a small village where the miner's children received an education. Hoge rebuilt a flour mill, sawmill, and blacksmith on the property and improved the bank barn and granary.

Also serving in politics, in 1877, Hoge held a Virginia Senate seat in Richmond, though this wouldn't stop his family suffering hardship, as two harsh winters were to follow. Their son Henry was born in December of 1878, and it was undoubtedly challenging to manage young children during the frigid winter. But Hoge's objective in politics was to promote the economic development of the Southwest. That is what he succeeded in doing. "He opened a whole new way of life for the Belsprings area" in which he lived. Land values from timber, minerals, and agriculture rose, as did livestock values. Belsprings was part of an economic boom. However, church and family were always the utmost priority for J. Hoge Tyler.

On Thursday, August 28, 1884, Hoge wrote in his diary, "God blessed us with another precious little daughter, born this morning at half-past six o'clock, and we named her Eleanor Howe Tyler, after my dear grandmother, and God grant she may grow up the same noble Christian woman she was." On June 28, 1885, Reverend S. R. Preston of Wytheville and Mr. Naff baptized both Eliza and Eleanor (Nellie). Eliza had been born September 12, 1882; however, she was sickly, and they thought they would lose her as an infant. The family prayed for her healing, and their prayers were answered. At three years old, she was baptized that evening at Belle-Hampton along with Nellie, who was almost one and very healthy at the time.

According to Hoge's diary dated April 18, 1886,

> ...our Darling little Nellie, She was taken to her Savior's arms at 9 o'clock last Thursday morning (15th), and we laid her in her little grave by the side of my Dear Grandmother. I dare not try to write my feelings; they have been awful grieved and depressed; despair has well nigh crushed me, but I thank God, I have been able to say, 'not my will but Thine be done.' Oh, how it had been my prayer, my hope, my belief, that all my darling children would be spared to me during my life. How blindly I had believed that this was God's promise to me! He had healed them all when sick, had answered every prayer I had made in their behalf, and crowned my life with richest blessings; had never withheld a good thing from me, but he could not let my darling remain with us; he loved it too much to leave it on earth, but wanted it for a little Angel, blessed thought. It was over ours on earth, for never was born a baby so angelic and so sweet; it was never anything but a joy to everybody and everything so patient, tender, and loving. God grant I may never have to make another sacrifice so great. But His will be done.

Nellie tragically died at almost two years old. Although Hoge does not say what little Nellie died from in his diary, a dissertation from 1969 notes that his two young daughters had typhoid, a bacterial infection from a type of Salmonella. Symptoms vary and can include mild to severe fever, headaches, and other aches and pains. Risk factors include poor sanitation and poor hygiene. Little Eliza did get better, but Nellie did not. Since sanitation seemed to be a cause, it is no wonder Tyler would later put in supposedly the first indoor bathroom in Pulaski County.

"Little Nellie" was memorialized with an angel statue gravestone. On her stone was a quote from Matthew 11:26, reading, "Even so father, for so it seemeth good in Thy sight." The interpretation of the passage is "God's will is the only rule of righteousness." She lies buried next to J. Hoge Tyler's grandmother's grave, her namesake, Eleanor Howe Hoge.

Little Nellie

Little Nellie, youngest daughter of Major J. Hoge Tyler of Pulaski County, Virginia, on last Thursday.

This is the first dark shadow that has ever fallen across that pleasant home. May God's grace be abundantly given his servants.

This sweet child used to say to her little sister, "Come and stay by me, Bud." May father, mother, brothers, and sisters all stand by her forever in the home of the blest.

"Perchance when the pearly gates unfold,
Her voice will be first to greet thine ear,
'Welcome, sweet mother home;'
And clasping thee with her tiny hand,
Thine angel child, 'mid a shining band.
Will lead thee to the throne."

Pastor

In 1891, the Tyler family left their ancestral home to move into their new home, Halwick, in Radford, VA. Did the heartbreak of losing his daughter at Belle-Hampton leave a black cloud over the property for Hoge, or was it his political ambition? Hoge became governor of Virginia in 1898, vacating Belle-Hampton as a primary residence forever, and his son Heth and his family only opened it as a summer home for over 100 years. Belle-Hampton spun into a downward spiral with the family's departure, leading it to become an abandoned, desolate structure hidden from the world. This was until fate intervened, when a descendant of the founder returned to resurrect the property. Although little Nellie's grave is still tucked away in the family cemetery, her short time on earth is not forgotten.

IN MEMORY
OF
AGNES SHANNON
Born June 46ᵗʰ 1851
Died July 17ᵗʰ 1852

On us in cruelty not in wrath
The Reaper came that day;
'Twas an angel visited the green earth
And took the flower away

CHAPTER 9

The Reaper and The Flowers

The Reaper and The Flowers
By Henry Longfellow, 1839

There is a Reaper, whose name is Death,
    And, with his sickle keen,
He reaps the bearded grain at a breath,
    And the flowers that grow between.

"Shall I have naught that is fair?" saith he;
    "Have naught but the bearded grain?
Though the breath of these flowers is sweet to me,
    I will give them all back again."

He gazed at the flowers with tearful eyes,
    He kissed their drooping leaves;
It was for the Lord of Paradise
    He bound them in his sheaves.

"My Lord has need of these flowerets gay,"
    The Reaper said, and smiled;
"Dear tokens of the earth are they,
    Where He was once a child.

"They shall all bloom in fields of light,
    Transplanted by my care,

Agnes Shannon b. June 15, 1851 d. July 14, 1852 (1 year)

And saints, upon their garments white,
   These sacred blossoms wear."

And the mother gave, in tears and pain,
   The flowers she most did love;
She knew she should find them all again
   In the fields of light above.

Oh, not in cruelty, not in wrath,
   The Reaper came that day;
'T was an angel visited the green earth,
   And took the flowers away.

ALTHOUGH MOST HOWE FAMILY MEMBERS stayed close to home in Virginia near the old homestead, Sunnyside, Major John Dunbar Howe's oldest daughter did not. Margaret Ann was born in Draper's Valley, but around the same time her family was moving to Sunnyside, she married Dr. George Shannon. She was 17 years old. They settled down in Newbern, VA, where she immediately got pregnant with their first child. Nine months after their wedding, their precious little daughter, Agnes, was born.

Little Agnes was still a baby when she passed away in the spring of 1852. The cause is unknown, but that year the nation fell foul to an epidemic of yellow fever, which may have been the culprit. Symptoms included fever, chills, loss of appetite, and nausea. After five days of improving, the fever would return with abdominal pain; this then led to liver damage, where you begin to see yellowing of the skin. As with most families, losing a child is heartbreaking, but was baby Agnes's death the cause for Margaret Ann Howe to leave Virginia? Maybe.

Memorialized on her daughter's stone was the last verse of Longfellow's poem,

> O, not in cruelty, not in wrath,
> The Reaper came that day;
> 'Twas an angel visited the green earth,
> And took the flowers away.

A timid, shy girl who was reluctant to move away from home must have had a reason to leave. A broken heart from a loss of a child was indeed justifiable. Texas was a strange new wildland but very prosperous

TO THE BELOVED
MEMORY OF
JOHN H. SHANNON.
Died
June 14, 1877,
Aged 22 years.

John H. Shannon, footstone

during the early years of statehood. For the young couple, the desire to start a new life after the tragic loss would have been an attractive venture.

Shortly after arriving in Texas, Margaret had another baby. This time it was a bouncing baby boy, who they named Johnny. But the dangers of motherhood combined with the raw wilderness of Texas didn't bode well for her. A couple of years after her son's birth, Margaret Ann Howe Shannon passed away, leaving her two-year-old son to be raised by his father. George Shannon returned to Virginia for only a short time before deciding to return to Texas with his young son. This time, it was to become a rancher.

Something attracted George to Texas's wide-open countryside, which was strikingly different from his Virginia home in the Shenandoah Valley. As his ranch prospered, his son would help out with the chores. As he grew, he was able to take on more responsibility. By age 22, Johnny could manage the steers on his own. But as cattlemen know, working with large animals can be a hazardous and dangerous job. As he was branding a steer one day, one broke loose and gored Johnny to death. A disturbing sight for anyone, but another tragedy for the Howe-Shannon family.

George returned to Sunnyside to bury his son alongside his sister in the family graveyard. For easy transportation of the body, he had him cremated. While George was making the funeral arrangements, he kept Johnny's remains in the west room of the house where he slept. The house was already filled with folk tales of ghosts who inhabited it, but the idea of remains kept inside—even temporarily—frightened the servants. Whispers about what lurked in the room upstairs kept the staff from entering the foreboding space. The incident gave rise to the many ghost stories that lasted for years to come.

The young children heard all the tales of Texas and the dangers of Indians, wild cowboys, and of course, steers that can gore you to death. Some humorous childhood beliefs developed during prayer time at John T. Howe's family household. The family already moved west from their homestead to Kansas about a year before their grandfather, Major John Dunbar Howe, passed away. Knowing about the stories of their uncle dying in Texas, the children conjured up all kinds of thoughts. While kneeling beside their chairs, the children would listen to their father read from the Bible every evening and then bow their heads in prayer. At the end of their prayers, their dad would always say, "And may the Lord watch over us and protect us." What seemed like an innocent statement was misinterpreted by the young children. Knowing all the tales of Texas together with their family's move to Kansas, they believed their father actually said, "And may the Lord watch over us in Texas." It always disturbed the young ones to assume their father was planning to move them there. For them, Texas was not in their life plan.

MAJ. JOHN D. HOWE

BORN
JAN. 4, 1801,
DIED
JAN. 9, 1885.

Gathered

CHAPTER 10

Wait for the Wagon

Around Our Father's Throne Above

Around our Father's throne above.
    In robes of spotless white.
An angel, in God's temple there,
    Who serves him day and night.
And in the crown which now he wears
    Shine stars, like jewels rare.
Placed there by loving deeds below,
    And tender thoughts and prayer;
An in his hands he bears the palm,
    Which only victor wave;
For he has triumphed over sin,
    Through Him who came to save.
An he shall never hunger now,
    Nor thirst in mid-days heat.
For by the Lamb he shall be fed,
    And brought to fountains sweet;
Nor shall he ever sorrow more,
    Nor feel the weight of fears,
For God himself shall comfort him
    And wipe away all tears.

—Lily Tyler, daughter of Governor
James Tyler Hoge, March 3, 1905

Maj. John Dunbar Howe b. January 4, 1801 d. January 9, 1885 (84 years)

IT WAS AN EXCITING PERIOD IN 1830 when John Dunbar Howe (29 years old) and Sarah Boyd Logan Shepherd (15 years old) were married. At that time, America boasted pride and a confident optimism because the future promised to be even better than the present. The couple settled down on a farm Sarah had inherited in the New Draper Valley (now Blacksburg), VA, from her father, Samuel Shepherd, who had passed away the year before. His youngest daughter, Sarah was recognized as "pretty and vivacious." She soon became pregnant and delivered a happy, healthy boy named Daniel after his grandfather, Maj. Daniel Howe. Unfortunately, the joy of their first years was crushed when they lost Daniel at only one and a half years old. The story of this young boy's life or even death went unrecorded.

Sadly, little Daniel's gravestone lay buried in pieces beneath the dirt. Unearthed in 2019 after being placed to rest 186 years earlier, the puzzle of who this grave belonged to began to be investigated. Although Daniel's gravestone had largely vanished over the years, the pieces that remained gave clues to whose grave it memorialized. A portion of the name *Howe* was evident. A chunk that looked to say *John* with another saying *son* seemed to conclude that it was Daniel's lost gravestone. A marker indicating German descent was curious. But we quickly realized that his great-great-grandmother was Maria Sophia Charlotte von Kielmansegg, Countess of Darlington and the half-sister of King George I. Daniel was a descendant from German royalty as well as British. The mystery is now solved.

For the young Howe family, more children quickly arrived. Their second child was born six months after the death of their son. It was a girl, named Margaret Ann. After their next two children, Susan and Eliza, were born in Draper's Meadows, the Howes decided to move to Newbern. The town laid out 29 lots along Wilderness Road with guaranteed access to the spring. It quickly began to prosper as a turnpike town, so John decided to open a mercantile business combined with a post office. Since it was part of the main stagecoach line from Baltimore to Nashville, it also served as a roadside tavern. Five more of his children were born in this newly formed town.

Before railroads and telegraphs became established, those that were anticipating letters or awaiting their newspapers would have to "wait for the wagon" before they were delivered. This situation was very beneficial for the mercantile business. General stores would keep a wide range of goods available for purchase, often staple food items such as milk and bread, and various household goods such as hardware and other

Sarah Boyd Logan Shepherd Howe b. August 20, 1815 d. March 22, 1859 (43 years)

supplies. As an astute owner, John would also keep liquor on hand for those not interested in shopping while waiting for the wagon. The use of this expression goes farther back than John's time, but he used it humorously on many occasions.

Even though he was successful in the now busy town, which had blacksmiths, tailors, carriage makers, doctors, cobblers, millers, and tanners, as well as a newspaper, John decided to move. He made a trade with his youngest brother, William, for the much-loved family house on Sunnyside. His brother had inherited that portion of the land, which included the cabin, when his father died in 1838. John's portion of the inheritance encompassed the location of the original homestead, which was no longer around. The third portion went to his other brother, Joseph. Here at his childhood home, John toiled as a farmer along with his loving wife, and they were blessed with two more children.

As industrial advancements came to Southwest Virginia, the excitement of the event in 1854 drew spectators from all around. John Thomas Howe, a boy of 12 at the time, recalled the first train pulling into Central Station, formerly named Lovely Mount. Waiting with as much anticipation as Christmas morning, John, along with his brother Harvey and cousin Jimmie Hoge Tyler, both seven years old, sat impatiently in their Sunday best clothes. His parents, John and Sarah, packed picnic baskets, which they spread under the maples near the depot. They consumed the food before any sight of a locomotive. But finally, they heard a distant roar, and someone shouted, "Here she comes." As the train slowed to a stop, the crowd gathered closer to ask the engineer and fireman questions while they cooled off, but they proceeded to turn the train around without further delay. After a dramatic display of smoke and sparks, the thunderous giant vanished in a cloud of silver steam. However, it started a dark time in the family as the story of the cemetery inhabitants unfolded.

The gravestone of William Harvey Howe sits broken next to his parents. The ninth child of eleven, William Harvey, along with two siblings, lays buried at Sunnyside. Heartbreakingly, they all passed away before their father. Etched into the stone is a rosebud reminding us of a fragile life that was tragically cut short. In 1857, there was one of the worst worldwide influenza epidemics. Although the cause of his death is unknown, he may have been a casualty of this illness. Although William was born in Draper's Meadows, now Blacksburg, he spent most of his short life enjoying the Howe homestead's sprawling pastures, Sunnyside. How fitting it is he would spend eternity overlooking those same fields. After losing a small child of eight years, not eighteen years, as noted on various family trees, his mourning parents decided to have another child, Agnes Shannon Howe. Tragically, Sarah Howe passed away just two short months after Agnes's birth, leaving nine children in the hands of her loving husband.

A worn discolored tombstone sits in the cemetery marking the burial site of Sarah Boyd Logan Shepherd Howe. Adorning the stone is a calla lily, symbolizing majestic beauty and marriage. Inscribed on her stone is the quote, "There will be rest in Heaven." Indeed, life at that time was strenuous, taking care of 11 children, sewing, weaving, knitting, supervising the servants, and ensuring "useful tasks were being done after chores" for all the children and servants. Did she live in constant fear of the Indians since her great-great-grandfather, Colonel James Patton, was killed in the horrific Indian massacre at Draper's Meadows? It would be reasonable to be anxious after losing three children and a grandchild; it might have been a burden too significant to bear on this earth.

In the end, she suffered considerably from dropsy either during or after giving birth to Agnes Shannon Howe (De Jarnette). This old term, dropsy, referred to the swelling of soft tissue due to excess water accumulation and described her experience of swelling to the face, ankles, and most likely, legs and hands. Little Agnes, named after George and Margaret Shannon's daughter buried at Sunnyside, was described as tiny, most

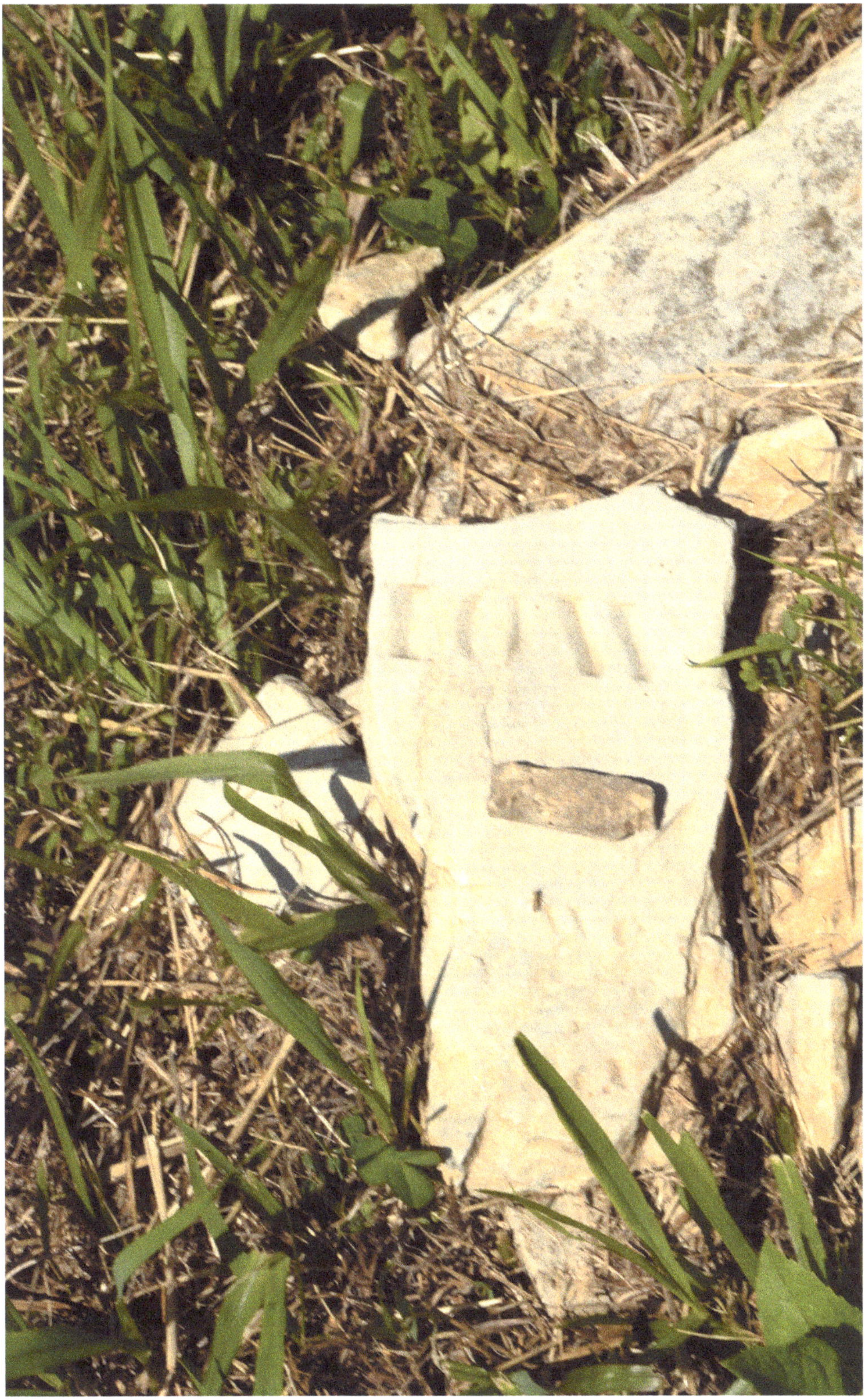

Gubless
Lynchburg

IN MEMORY OF
WILLIAM HARVEY HOWE
Son of John D. & Sarah R. Howe
Born
Augt 10, 1849

likely premature birth. Agnes lived to 75, although she too lost a baby, called Agnes. Sarah now rests in peace with her daughter, sons, and granddaughter in heaven (see the Shannon family's story).

Although John Howe's family's stories in the cemetery might end there, the worst was still to come when the world split apart in 1861, dividing the North and the South into a Civil War. John would have been in his sixties and too old to fight. The average soldier's age was between 18–30 years old. John's sons, John Thomas, Samuel Shepherd, and eventually Haven Boyd Howe all served as Confederate soldiers.

On the morning of April 15, 1861, President Lincoln issued action to invade the south. That day changed the Howe family's life forever. The Northern aggression, considered fighting words in the south, prompted John Thomas Howe to enlist in the Fourth Virginia Volunteer Infantry Regiment in Blacksburg. The perception at that time was that the troops were embarking on a great adventure with grand experiences, but what was in store for them was an unforeseen tragedy.

John entered the war and missed the Battle of Bull Run due to illness, but he later joined the Battle of Sharpsburg (Antietam), the bloodiest battle in the war, where General Lee's only course of action was an early withdrawal. Lee later said he was most proud of this battle because he believed his men faced the heaviest odds invading in the Union theater. It was the first threat from the Confederates so close to Washington D.C. He took a new defensive position along the hills east of Martinsburg, MD, which turned out to be a failed tactic. After the Union's victory, a turning point in the war, Lincoln had the confidence to issue the Emancipation Proclamation on January 1, 1863. With the combination of the proclamation and their defeat at Antietam, the first battle on Northern soil, the Southern troops' hopes were dampened. However, they still perceived they could achieve their goal by avoiding defeat.

Samuel Shepherd joined the Confederates in Martinsburg among the weary troops on September 25, 1862. He united with his brother, now Lt. John T. Howe, in the Fourth Virginia Volunteer Infantry Regiment. There's no mention of him actually volunteering since he probably became drafted after turning 18 in August of that year. The new Confederate Congress passed the Conscription Act in April of 1862, stating that all able-bodied men from 18–35 should serve. Fredricksburg was Samuel's first battle.

In the early morning with a heavy rain, Union troops had difficulty crossing the Rappahannock due to the heavy fog, hindering their attack. Lee's troops occupied the high ground in anticipation of the battle.

The southern forces were waiting with "stubborn resolution" after receiving substantial reinforcements. While watching the Union soldiers march bravely into battle in near faultless order, onlookers noted how magnificent it looked: "Their bright bayonets glistening in the sunlight made the line look like a huge serpent of blue and steel . . ." While a stone wall shielded the Confederate infantry, the Union soldiers were slaughtered or wounded, making it difficult to survive through the cold December night. The carnage devastated the ranks as well as Lincoln back in Washington. Samuel, however, along with his comrades, felt the thrill of victory.

There was a lull between the two storms of battle, but after the cold winter months of careful waiting, the Fourth Virginia Regiment troops made their historic march to Chancellorsville through the wilderness. The inactivity would have been relaxing were it not for the brutal winter, bringing with it disease, malnutrition, and exposure to the elements. Because of the poor conditions of the troops, Lee needed to remain defensive. However, the Union camp's situation appeared worse, with a wave of deserters prompting Lincoln to put "Fighting Joe" Hooker in charge. Hooker did not want another battle of Fredericksburg, so he carefully planned to outmaneuver Lee, recorded as saying, "My plans are perfect, and when I start to carry them out, may God have mercy on General Lee, for I will have none."

Although Hooker had a plan, he didn't account for the terrain's heavy thicket and raw wilderness. Trying to outflank Lee, he tried to come from behind, but Lee called his bluff by moving from his defensive position in Fredericksburg to Chancellorsville. With the help of General Stonewall Jackson, Lee's troops drove Hooker to withdraw forces back across the river. Lee had little time to relish in the triumph though. Since his troops suffered more losses than the Unionists, he knew he couldn't continue to endure these considerable casualties. The general decided to go on the offensive and move north, but Stonewall Jackson died in the meantime. The loss of their distinguished leader became the battle cry for their next encounter, "Charge, boys and remember Jackson."

Samuel Howe and the fourth infantry fought in that historic battle. Although victorious, it was also significant since they witnessed General Stonewall Jackson's demise. As recorded in history, Jackson was shot in the confusion of the battle by friendly fire. Struck by three rifle balls, Jackson required surgery to amputate his arm and later died from pneumonia, much to the shock of his worshipful Stonewall Brigade.

Determined to intimidate and demoralize the Unionists, Lee decided to proceed north into enemy territory by crossing first into Maryland,

SAMUEL SHEPHERD HOWE
SON OF
JOHN D. & SARAH B. HOWE
Born Aug. 20, 1844
Died at Point Lookout, Md.
Aug. 14, 1864

He was brought home and buried
in the family Graveyard May
___ 1866. And to his memory this
marble slab has been Erected by
aged and sorrowing Father

None knew him, but to love him,
None named him, but to praise.

Address, &c.
Lynchbrg.

then into Pennsylvania, not foreseeing the monumental struggles that would emerge in Gettysburg. The veterans of the Stonewall Brigade knew that a great campaign was underway. Spirits were high in anticipation of a successful mission. Their uniting cry,

> "Rally around the flag, boys, rally once again,
> Shout out the battle cry of free-ee-dom!"

Ordered not to loot, vandalize, or destruct property for retaliation purposes as they moved onto northern soil, the Confederate soldiers received specific instruction to instead requisition cattle, grain, hay, and other provisions to fulfill the needs of the troops. This order fell on deaf ears as they ransacked farms and stores, seizing property with no reimbursement record, much like the Federalists did in the south.

As the Confederate Infantry made its way to Gettysburg, they were unaware of the Union soldiers' location. When they inadvertently ran into a small Union Calvary on their search for shoes, Lee ordered General Richard Ewell to take the hill "if practicable." Ewell held back, lacking the courage to proceed. Although a Rebel victory seemed apparent by day's end with the Union's retreat, history records Ewell as to blame for losing the battle since he had failed to pursue the defeated Northern army.

Day two demonstrated the Union's most legendary episodes of the war. Brutal fighting took place at Devil's Den, where boulders wouldn't permit any organized formation, thus creating jumbled forces traversing rugged terrain in unbearably hot weather. One of the Howe's cousins and James Fulton Hoge's son, Andrew Johnson Hoge, a sharpshooter, was killed on that day during the intense fighting in the Devil's Den. Remarkably, the Federalists, after running out of ammunition, bayonet charged their way up Little Round Top to keep the Rebels off vital high ground, spoiling Lee's unwavering plan of success.

On the third day of the battle, July 3, 1863, the two Howe brothers participated in the tragic "Pickett's Charge." Now promoted to a captain, John T. Howe led Company E of the Fourth Virginia Volunteers to charge courageously across an open stretch of 1,400 yards. Bravely dodging through musket fire, iron balls bound together fired from heavy cannons, and tinned iron cans containing lead balls that scattered when fired, the young lads followed the order.

"My brave Virginians are to attack in front. Oh, may God in mercy help me as He never helped before," General George Pickett proclaimed before entering the battle. Captain John T. Howe led the squad to seek cover behind a stone fence, but the wall was hit by a shell, causing the captain to blackout. Once regaining consciousness, he observed his younger brother, Samuel, severely wounded with other brave souls who lay lifeless and mangled. Captain Howe was severely shaken, but his leg wound prevented him from moving. Instantly he knew the fate of himself and his brother; they were in the hands of the enemy.

After a brief stay at a field hospital for his injuries from the Battle of Gettysburg, Samuel Shepherd Howe was taken captive and held in Maryland as a Union prisoner of war. Point Lookout, MD, emerged to house the largest prisoner population but soon became the worst camp due to the squalid conditions. The camp was overcrowded, with tents and shacks instead of barracks. These left the prisoners open to the elements, with coastal storms often flooding their tents. Freshwater for drinking was scarce, and food became adamantly rationed. Besides inadequate food, clothing, fuel, housing, and medical assistance, over 3,000 prisoners died from chronic diarrhea, dysentery, typhoid fever, smallpox, or scurvy within 22 months. Samuel couldn't escape the plague of diseases. Only after a year in prison, he died unceremoniously for his service. His ashes were then returned to his homestead on Sunnyside. The epitaph on the tombstone told his story:

> Samuel Shepherd Howe
> Son of John D. and Sarah B. Howe
> Born August 20, 1844
> Died at Point Lookout, Maryland August 14, 1864
> He was brought home and buried in the family
> Graveyard, March 2, 1866. And to his memory
> The marble slab has been erected by his aged
> And sorrowing father.
>
> None know him, but to love him,
> None named him, thee to praise.

Also captured by the enemy, Captain John T. Howe was nursed back to health and eventually released from military prison in around 1864, enabling him to resume as a leader of his troops. But at the Appomattox Court House in 1865, he received his official stamped document releasing him from service. After receiving his personal belongings, including his uniform, personal equipment, and overcoat, Captain John Howe left for home. A benefit restricted to officers, he also received a horse. His recollection of arriving home went as follows: "Upon arrival at Sunnyside, the family rushed out on the lawn to greet me, and then I sat down on the porch to cool off and refresh myself with a drink of icy cold water brought direct from the spring house. The folks gathered around to hear all about the last days fighting, the surrender at Appomattox Court House, and my trip home." After the war, he settled down as a quiet farmer in Montgomery County.

After serving in the Virginia Cavalry until the end of the war, Haven Boyd Howe also returned home to his family. He would tell tales of the Battles of Milford, Dinwiddie Court House, and Five Forks. The family spent endless hours in lively conversation discussing what had transpired over the past four years. He eventually settled down with his new wife, Catherine McGavock Cloyd, and began, as others in the area, a thriving cattle business. The railroads caused dramatic growth for his enterprise, which enabled him to build an elaborate high-style Victorian home, now a museum called the Haven B. Howe House.

Major John Dunbar lived for another 20 years after he buried his son Samuel and the return of his other two sons from "The War Between the States." The heartbreak of burying his wife, a daughter, two sons, and a granddaughter came to an end when he was buried beside them all. The year was 1885 when he passed away, just five days after his 84th birthday. He lived a full and eventful life on his Sunnyside property overlooking Back Creek. As he would say, "Wait for the wagon," and his wagon came that day.

OUR DARLING

ELLEN DUNBAR HOWE
DIED
Dec. 8. 1874.
Aged 7 Mo. & 2 Days.

CHAPTER 11

War Is More Bearable Than Peace

Gone to the rest of the ever blest
To the new Jerusalem
Where the children of light do walk in white
And the Saviour leadeth them

For ever gone and none to mourn
And who for me would sorrow
I came to toil in a desert soil
And my task will be done tomorrow

—Passion Flowers: Mortal and Immortal,
Julia Ward Howe, 1854

AFTER THE CIVIL WAR ENDED, Captain John T. Howe returned to his family's homestead alive, but no longer an optimistic youth. Only 23 years old, his outlook was now that of pessimism. A returning soldier from the South described the situation as the following: "War is more bearable than peace." The area was poverty-stricken since Yankee soldiers ravaged the farms, draining livestock, crops, and other supplies before burning everything in their path. It was no longer safe after dark to keep chickens or contents of smokehouses protected from thieves in the lawless aftermath. With only minimal provisions left over after the war, supplies were stripped by poachers from the hard-working farmers of the South during this reconstruction period. Although they were gradually drifting into "respectable poverty," they kept their heads high and tried to return to their courtly Southern traditions.

A timely wedding announcement arrived as a promising celebration. What turned out to be the social event of the day, Major Chapman Snidow, grandson of famed Revolutionary War soldier Col. Christian Snidow, and Ann Eliza, the oldest daughter of James Fulton Hoge, were engaged. It would be the first ceremony since the dispiriting end of the war. As the planning for the event of the season progressed, the groom asked Captain John Howe to be a groomsman. Simultaneously, Ann Eliza Hoge asked Sallie De Jarnette, a relative, to be her bridesmaid. Only 18 at the time, Sallie had never met John before since she was off at Grosse's Finishing School in Albemarle County during the war. A romance quickly ensued, much to the dismay of Sallie's family.

The De Jarnettes were from Caroline County in Northern Virginia. Described at the time as the wild and uncivilized west, Southwest Virginia would not be considered a place for a young, sophisticated lady such as Sallie. In fact, her family was even fearful that Indians might attack her. Undoubtedly, they had heard about the Draper's Meadows raid and the Mary Ingles story. Despite this, the budding lovers performed their vows on June 13, 1866, at Clifton in Caroline County. Reverend James C. Parish officiated the service, where their families came together to rejoice in the festivities.

After the celebration was over, Captain John T. Howe and Sallie (De Jarnette) Howe moved to the tarnished red "Riverton" farmhouse located in Montgomery County. The 283 acres which fronted the New River was John's inheritance from ancestral landholdings. Serendipitously, this was the same farm where John's grandfather met his wife almost a century before (see Major Daniel Howe). The brick dwelling replaced the original log cabin, but the tales of his grandparents' epic romantic encounter continue to live on in family history.

However, Sallie lived a life accustomed to the finer things, a far cry from the hardships of the farm. Being raised in a home where she never touched her hand in dishwater, Sallie had every need cared for before her marriage. She didn't even do her own hair, since she was assigned a maid to take care of those personal chores. They had a cook, houseboy, and regular servants at her home in Caroline County to attend to the

OUR PET

BESSIE DEJARNET
HOWE
DIED
Feb. 12, 1874
Aged 2 Y.

family. A girl of the southern aristocracy would not even consider doing the housework of any kind during the antebellum days. She was to spend time with needlework, music, and the arts, whereas servants were to do everything classified as work or manual labor. Not only did life change for every southern girl from the pre-Civil War days, but marriage also brought another dimension of responsibilities and heartbreaks.

Children quickly came into the picture, Sallie giving birth to their first son, Robert, in March of 1867, nine months after their marriage. One would presume she would have received help from her mother, Cordelia, had she not passed away the year Sallie married. Maybe her sister Jane, came to assist? But Jane's second baby was that same year. Sallie's father married Cordelia's sister, Margaret (Peggy), in April of 1867, just a month after Robert's birth. Perhaps it was Aunt Peggy, as Margaret was known, who helped Sallie with her first baby, although that seems unlikely so close to the wedding. Her first baby must have been difficult with no help from servants or family to assist her.

The next year, Sallie gave birth to Samuel at John's ancestral home, Sunnyside. But who helped Sallie with the delivery is unknown. Her mother-in-law, Sarah Boyd Logan Shepherd, had died shortly after giving birth to her daughter Agnes in 1859. Her father-in-law never remarried. But John's sister Minnie (Minnesota) might have been there to help, as she was still living at home—though she would have only been 16 years old. John's other sisters were tending to their own families but may have been available. Ellen Mary (Howe) Kent lived at "Oakshade" in Dublin, so she was not too far away to help her brother's wife deliver.

Sallie and John's next child, Ellen, was the first child born at Riverton. But continuing the hardship of post-war devastation, at seven months, her daughter died of croup and pneumonia. Adorned on her gravestone is a dove, which symbolizes purity and peace along with the inscription "Our Darling." After a thorough clean in 2018, her stone glistens in the sunlight, memorializing the innocent life lost before it even began. Sallie was not only experiencing the misfortune of the new kind of world she found herself in; losing a child brought on the grief of death. A sure test of her perseverance.

Her dreams evaporated quickly with the mourning of the loss of her daughter combined with the labors, which required her to go from sunrise to sunset with steady cooking and cleaning tasks. Since she weighed no more than 100 pounds, her frail physique required necessary fortitude and adaptability. Through her challenging experiences, she became resourceful and determined to make their house their home, with the southern traditions driving her forward. But other challenges were still ahead for the young couple.

Born almost a year after her sister died, Bessie De Jarnette blessed the family with her arrival on a cold December day. They were grateful for another healthy child but were unaware life on the farm would quickly go from bad to worse. Already burdened with debt and the demonetization of silver in 1873, which caused a widespread depression, their cash was limited. The farm's operations required money, so John looked to sell his family farm, Riverton. After a trip to Chicago to secure an agreement, John received a questionable deal with a buyer involving stocks as a payment. The agreement was halted due to the uncertainty of the market. Since other matters were more urgent on the farm, the decision was made to take the farm off the market for the time being.

The fall season quickly approached, which was hog-killing time. This essential annual farm task required everyone's participation. The first chore was to kill the hogs. Next, the men hauled the hogs down to the river, where tanks positioned in the dirt at ground level held boiling water. The hogs could then be easily lowered into the tanks of scalding water to cook. Afterward, the women made sausage, liver pudding, and pickled pork from the meat. Hog killing was arduous work for all involved.

Sallie, however, just the day before, had errands to run in Christiansburg. They needed household supplies and fall clothes for the growing children. The chills of a November day were good reminders of the necessity of warm clothes. She brought her "pet," three-year-old Bessie, with her into town. Tales of little red riding hood must have intrigued little Bessie (or Sallie) since she returned home with a hood of her own. A bright red riding hood suit and shoes to match was the adorable child's outfit of choice.

Anxious to show off her new attire, Bessie came out that chilly Tuesday morning beautifully dressed. The household was already bustling with hog killing and cooking. Sallie had Johnny to attend to since he was a lively nine-month-old baby. She suggested Bessie should show off her new outfit to her brothers, assumed to be playing just outside the house. But Bob (Robert), seven years old, and Shepherd (Samuel), six years old, had wandered further from the house to swing on the grapevines. They were also curious about the hog operations and hoped to catch a glimpse. Bessie, filled with jubilation in her new outfit, sprang out the door in search for her brothers.

As Bessie headed in the direction of her brothers playing, Shep yelled and gestured with his arms for her to go back. Instead of turning around,

Bessie saw his waving arms as an invitation to come and play. Oblivious to the hidden dangers, Bessie skipped gleefully forward. Her brothers frantically tried to swing and run out to stop her. But she already reached the vat, tripping over the sacks surrounding it and plunging directly into the scalding hot water. Both of her brothers tried frantically to lift her out, but they did not have the strength. "Aunt" Caroline, who heard the screams, jumped out the window with no regard to her own safety and pulled out the child.

As other members of the family arrived to carry her to the house, Bessie's only complaint was that "her finger hurt so badly." Since she held onto the tank so hard, it was only her fingers that didn't get immersed in the water. Any efforts for her to recover or prayers to save her were useless. The dear sweet child died within the hour, quietly in peace.

"My Pet" is inscribed on the top of her tombstone and surrounded by flowers. Bessie De Jarnette Howe, her death date of November 17, 1874, and her age of 2 years, 11 months were the only other things etched in the stone. She was buried next to her sister, Ellen, in the cemetery. Her mother was so broken-hearted, John knew the family needed immediate change.

One week after the funeral, John bought a farm in Blacksburg where they built a house called "King's Spring." He contacted the buyer that was previously interested in Riverton to sell it to them even with the risky terms. In March 1875, the Howe family packed up their belongings, never again to return to the place where so many tragedies in their life occurred. Blacksburg was the promised land, or so they thought. After enduring so many sorrows, they were eternally optimistic about what their future would bring.

Born
May 29, 1822
Died
Feb 8, 1885

CHAPTER 12

A Life of Service, Knowledge, and Family

So When a Great Man Dies

"Death takes us by surprise,
And stays our hurrying feet;
The great design unfinished lies,
Our lives are incomplete.

But in the dark unknown,
Perfect their circles seem,
Even as a bridge's arch of stone
Is rounded in the stream.

Alike are life and death,
When life in death survives,
And the uninterrupted breath
Inspires a thousand lives.

Were a star quenched on high,
For ages would its light,
Still traveling downward from the sky,
Shine on our mortal sight.

Dr. William and Jane Hoge

So when a great man dies,
For years beyond our ken,
The light he leaves behind him lies
Upon the paths of men."

—Henry Wadsworth Longfellow, 1875

ON A CLEAR SPRING DAY, my husband, Tom, and our boys, Tyler, Peyton, and Mason, along with myself, trekked over to Sunnyside to begin the laborious task of clearing the cemetery, thus honoring its inhabitants. Among the graves, a tumbled obelisk laid face down in the dirt covering the name of who was buried there. As the day wore on and the place was cleared of overgrown weeds, we decided to turn over the large marker to discover the resident of the grave. Our son, William Hoge, who goes by his middle name, Mason, was up for the challenge and heavy lifting. Once the stone was turned, we wiped the dirt and debris off the inscription. To our surprise, it was Dr. William Hoge's stone. However, it was surreal to find his birthday, May 26, matched our son's birthday as well. One hundred and seventy-one years apart, the two William's share more than the ground beneath their feet, and Young William has honored his ancestor and namesake by revealing this marker's owner. But it wasn't until July 4th of that year that we lifted the obelisk to an upright position, securing it on its base. It took seven Hoge men, ancestors of William, to wrestle the stone into place. Once erect, we properly cleaned the stone and placed an American flag by it to honor his service in the Civil War.

Having revealed the name, the life story of William was still to be unearthed—and would prove a much greater find. Born at Hayfield in Montgomery County (now Pulaski County), VA, William lived in a small cabin built by his grandfather, James Mayo Hoge. He is the youngest son of General James and Eleanor Hoge. When William arrived into the world, his mother was 29 years old, and his father, 38, had already earned distinguished service in the military. William received the finest education, which led to his career as a medical doctor. And like his father, he was always meticulously dressed and road the finest horses.

On the opposite side of the obelisk is the engraving for William's wife, Jane Meek. She was born in Washington County, VA, at Hope Manor in Glade Spring, an Indian word meaning "this is the place," located about 80 miles from where William grew up. Jane is the eldest child of 11 from James and Jestiana Meek, although technically second oldest since her

DR. WM E. HOGE

BORN

MAY 26, 1822

DIED

FEB. 6, 1885

brother died before she was born. She received the finest education by attending Salem College in North Carolina, the oldest private women's liberal arts establishment in the United States (founded in 1772), where she became well versed in Latin. Her father, James, being a successful, wealthy man, bought 2,240 acres in the heart of Burke's Garden, known as "God's thumbprint" due to its bowl-shaped crater terrain. Traveling by horse and buggy with $20,500 of gold in his buckboard, he successful purchased the property for about $9 an acre at auction. Unfortunately, his untimely death, blamed on eating too much corn (twelve ears), didn't allow him to enjoy his acquisition. His demise was attributed to the family lore that one should eat no more than three ears of corn per helping. However, the true reason for his death was most likely a heart attack from his long, stressful journey to obtain the purchase.

Prior to her father's death, Jane married William in her town at Glade Spring. They lived with William's parents at Hayfield in the early years of their marriage. The main brick house had been completed 20 years prior, with plenty of room for them and their soon-to-be growing family. Only 11 months later, they had their first child, Eleanor Jestiana, named after both mothers, although she went by Ellen. The couple's choice to live with William's parents may have been out of necessity. Eliza, William's sister, passed away in childbirth, leaving baby James Hoge Tyler to be raised by his grandparents. Although little James also had a wet nurse, Sarah, surely having William and Jane around as well as their young family would have been a benefit for all. Only one year later, in 1847, James Meek arrived. Although one would think it might be confusing to have both James Hoge Tyler and James Meek Hoge running around together, we later found that young Tyler went by his middle name, Hoge.

Babies continued to arrive, six in all. The last ones being Robert Sayer, Eliza, William Howe, and Olivia. She passed away at 27 days old. Her little gravestone is adorned with a calla lily, reflecting a life of faith, purity, and holiness. The quote on the stone reads, "Of such is the Kingdom of Heaven."

Then, only two months after William was born, Ellen (Eleanor Jestiana) passed away. Then, on September 16, 1853, only two months after William was born, Ellen (Eleanor Jestiana) passed away. She was eight years and two months old. We are not sure of the cause, but yellow fever was prevalent in America at that time. Did this event inspire William to open a medical practice in Newbern around 1855?

Sadly, like little Eliza, the only record of Ellen's life is inscribed on a little gravestone adorned with a calla lily with the quote:

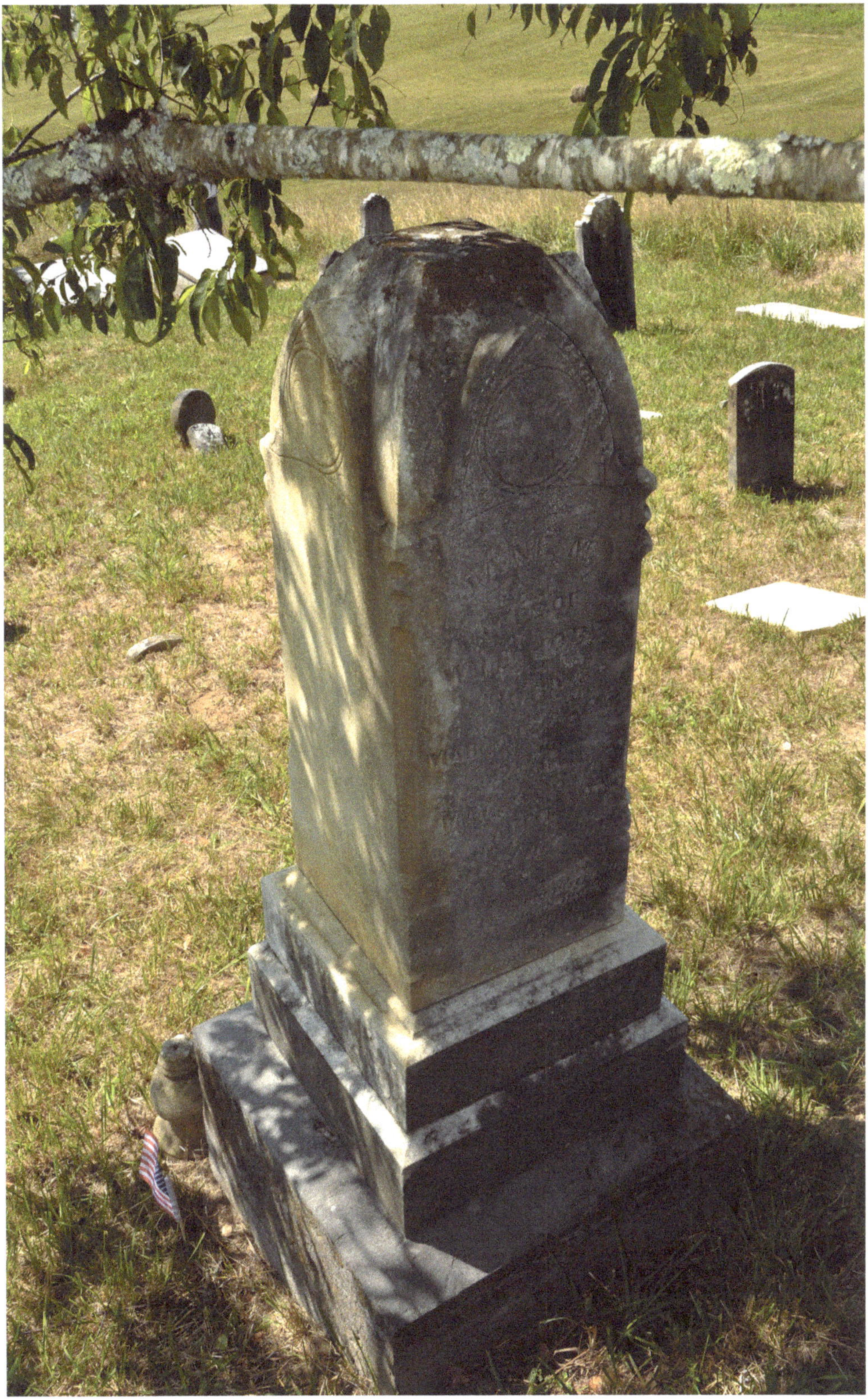

ELLEN JESTIANNA
Daughter of Wm E. & Jane Hoge,
who died Sept. 16, 1853;
aged 8 years, 2 mo's, & 19 days

She was lovely, she was fair,
And for a while was given;
An angel came and claimed his own
And bore her home to heaven.

Eliza Hoge b. Oct. 25, 1851 d. Nov. 21, 1851 (27 days)

> She was lovely, she was fair,
> And for a while was given:
> An angel came and claimed his own
> And bore her home to heaven.

The grief continued for the household when William suddenly lost his mother to a heart attack on the front stairs overlooking the valley just a few years later. The decade leading up to the Civil War, politicians battled through the turmoil of the nation all while the Hoge family mourned the continuous loss of its family members. Almost 10 died and were buried in the cemetery just in that decade alone—a loss greater than in the war itself.

Somewhere after the decade came to a close, William and Jane moved to Point Pleasant, VA, also called the Slide. Still to this day it is considered the most beautiful piece of property in Bland County. Jane most likely inherited it after her father's sudden passing, but since he didn't have a will, it took almost a decade to settle the estate. During these turbulent times, they hardly had time to enjoy their new life before William was called to serve in the Civil War. As a doctor for the Confederate army, he witnessed the most gruesome injuries with limited tools to assist the wounded. A typical toolkit included a capital saw, a rongeur (used to cut bone), a tourniquet, two trephines (hole saws used to remove circles of

Eleanor (Ellen) Justina Hoge b. Jul. 16, 1845 d. Sep. 16, 1853 (8 years, 2 months)

tissue or bone), two knives, four pairs of tweezers, a director, a lancet, and a Hey's saw (used for cranial resections). In particular, the Battle of Cloyd's Mountain, which lasted only an hour with most of it hand-to-hand combat, contained some of the most severe and savage fighting of the war. William was there for the repairs. It affected him so much that his medical practice never accepted a payment for services rendered.

During the war, Eleanor S. Hoge came to live at their property. She was the daughter of George and Rebecca Pearis Hoge, the former of which was John and Elizabeth Rippy's son. Rebecca was the granddaughter of Capt. George Pearis, whose name founded Pearisburg. Eleanor S. Hoge previously lived with her family in Pearisburg, which was described as noisy, unpredictable, and disruptive, and the war activities agitated the once-calm rural air and changed the lives of Southwest Virginians. After the brutality of the Battle of Cloyd's Mountain and losing her father just before the war, she escaped to the safety of William's family until her marriage to James Robinett when she was 17 years old. Eleanor would surely have been a blessing for the family after the loss of their daughter Ellen, who would have been a similar age had she survived.

When the war ended in 1865, along with the other Confederate soldiers, William received amnesty, leaving him to establish a new life for Jane and himself. William continued with his core value of service by becoming a Freemason, rising to the level of First Worshipful Master. He reestablished his medical practice, performing an appendectomy on one patient, which was very advanced medicine at the time. However, he specialized in cases of diphtheria, a serious and dangerous infection affecting children at that time. He continued to farm on his beautiful property in Burke's Garden, VA, where he could pursue his passion for horses. Jane and William's love for learning evolved into an extensive library in their home. They lived their core values of service and knowledge, but their main guiding principle was family.

Jane and William became guardians to their niece and nephew, Sophia and Eugene, when they were only five and three years old. Jane's sister Sophia and her husband, Henry Edmondson, along with their son Tommie, died from yellow fever in 1878 leaving the children as orphans. They were living in Memphis, TN, when a major outbreak occurred there. 25,000 residents fled the city in two weeks. Of those that stayed, 2,000 people died horrific deaths. Officials posted checkpoints at major locations in the city trying to quarantine the residents. Risking his personal health, William, being a doctor, was able to ride into town to retrieve the two children. However, he had to smuggle them out of the city under his buggy seat. He then traveled to the home of their grandmother, Jane's mom, Jestiana, in Broadford, VA, 550 miles away. After a brief stop, he then continued another 50 miles to Bland County before they were safe at home. Since the children and William were all potentially exposed to the fever, neighbors resented his heroic deed for fear of a local outbreak. But for William, taking care of his family was more important than the possible exposure.

On a trip to Wytheville, VA, William met his untimely death at 62 years old. Although he was previously stricken by paralysis, he recovered. This time as he returned home on February 3, 1885, he became incapacitated again and died at a gentlemen's home along his route. This left Jane to raise her niece and nephew, now 10 and 12 years old. Their daughter Olivia moved with her husband, Colonel James S. Browning, to Richmond, Virginia, and started her own family. Olivia's second daughter, Rebecca, was only one at the time. Jane lived nine more years after her husband died in Burke's Garden, VA.

Jane's body was the last to be buried in the Sunnyside Cemetery, in 1894. Because they were not living in the area when they passed away, I often wonder why William and Jane were brought back to the family burial ground. Maybe they wanted to be laid to rest next to their two small children and William's parents. Or it could be that their view of the peaceful countryside would provide them eternal peace. Whatever the reason, they are now sleeping in the valley where the mockingbird sings over their graves.

The Belle-Hampton Witness Tree, Black Walnut, 2017

Still Think of Me

When at the still quiet hours of twilight
Seated beneath some long loved steady tree,
You pensive more upon the coming night:
It is the hour I love—then think of me

When far abroad you wander to admire,
The work of God which all around you see,
And your soul is filled with heavenly fire,
Tis my delight—O then remember me.

When in your closet bowed before your God
You pray, and none around to hear or see
That God who shakes creation with his nod
Will hear your humble prayer—think then of me.

Where're you be, I still your love will claim
For I will fondly still remember thee
Though far apart I will still be the same
O will you not my friend—still think of me.

—Eliza Hoge (Tyler)
Back Creek, Dec. 28, 1835

Belle-Hampton Main House, 2020

Madeline S. Hoge, Author

John Naylor, Photographer

www.belle-hampton.com

Printed in the USA
CPSIA information can be obtained
at www.ICGtesting.com
LVHW061158171223
766671LV00042B/1580